American Immigration: A Very Short Introduction

Very Short Introductions available now:

For more information visit our web site
www.oup.com/vsi/

David A. Gerber

AMERICAN IMMIGRATION

A Very Short Introduction

OXFORD
UNIVERSITY PRESS

Oxford University Press, Inc., publishes works that further
Oxford University's objective of excellence
in research, scholarship, and education.

Oxford   New York
Auckland   Cape Town   Dar es Salaam   Hong Kong   Karachi
Kuala Lumpur   Madrid   Melbourne   Mexico City   Nairobi
New Delhi   Shanghai   Taipei   Toronto

With offices in
Argentina   Austria   Brazil   Chile   Czech Republic   France   Greece
Guatemala   Hungary   Italy   Japan   Poland   Portugal   Singapore
South Korea   Switzerland   Thailand   Turkey   Ukraine   Vietnam

Published by Oxford University Press, Inc.
198 Madison Avenue, New York, NY 10016

www.oup.com

Library of Congress Cataloging-in-Publication Data
Gerber, David A., 1944–
American immigration : a very short introduction / David A. Gerber.
p. cm.— (Very short introductions)
Includes bibliographical references.
ISBN 978-0-19-533178-3 (pbk.)
1. United States—Emigration and immigration.
2. United States—Emigration and immigration—History.
3. Cultural pluralism—United States.   I. Title.
JV6465.G47 2011
304.8'73—dc22   2010042520

7 9 8

Printed in Great Britain
by Ashford Colour Press Ltd., Gosport, Hants.
on acid-free paper

For Chris, Valerie, and Jaylyn

Contents

List of illustrations

Introduction: mass immigration, past and present

The United States is a nation of diverse peoples, formed not through a common genealogy, as were its European counterparts among capitalist democracies. Instead, its people have been bound together through allegiances to a constitution, outlining the framework for the making of law and for governance, and a loosely defined, ever contested creed. Americans are moved to love their country not by language that speaks of membership in an "American family," but rather by the powerful rhetorical formulations of Jefferson's *Declaration of Independence* that establish the promise of "life, liberty, and the pursuit of happiness." What this inspiring language means in practice is an ongoing argument that holds Americans together.

America's diverse peoples have come from every corner of the globe. They have been brought together by a number of historical processes—conquest, colonialism, a slave trade, territorial acquisition, and voluntary international migrations—that involve profound differences of volition and hardly amount to common experience. Of these processes, none looms larger in the American imagination than voluntary immigration, upon which one especially resonant myth of American origins has been based. That myth establishes that Americans did not become a nation by accident. Instead, they exercised a choice, even if one frequently conceived within crushing poverty, based on their appraisal of the

1

superior American form of government and of the American creed. The Founding Fathers' agreement to unify the thirteen original colonies into a nation-state was and still is complemented by the choice of those who opted to live in the democratic republic the founders established, and who swear allegiance to it by becoming citizens.

Since its founding in 1789, the United States has experienced almost constant immigration, but especially noteworthy have been three massive waves of voluntary international migration that reconfigured the population: (1) in the 1840s and 1850s, (2) from the late 1890s to World War I, and (3) in recent decades, dating from changes in American immigration law in 1965. Throughout its history, immigrants have been understood primarily as an economic asset. Not only did immigrant farmers help populate the interior, but the economy has also had a voracious appetite for immigrant wage labor. Immigrant labor has many advantages as a reserve source of workers: it may fill the need for specialized workers for proscribed periods of time; it may be repatriated or repatriate itself when times are bad; the costs of training and education have been assumed in the immigrant's homeland; and there are not necessarily any social welfare obligations, such as compensation for injury, on the part of the employer or the state. In addition, hiring friends and family of low-wage immigrant labor, as opposed to expensive formal recruiting of workers, has enabled employers easily to reproduce a cheap, expendable work force.

Approximately 35 million of 50 million Europeans who emigrated from their homelands in search of opportunity and material security between 1820 and 1920 came to the United States. Added to that immense number during the same century must be at least another million, even harder to count accurately, from Asia and Mexico, Canada and elsewhere in the Western Hemisphere. The first two waves of immigration came amid the transition of the United States from a rural, agrarian society to an urban, industrial one. Immigrants supplied the reserves of cheap labor that enabled this transition to take place. From that century images of the Irish ditch digger, Polish steelworker, Slovak coal miner, Jewish garment worker, and Italian construction worker are enshrined in American memory. Less well represented in the imagination, but significant, especially in the American West, are the Mexican agricultural worker, the Japanese market farmer, and the Chinese railroad construction laborer, though the numbers of people never equaled the numbers of Europeans in the historic past.

Changes in the immigration laws in 1965 opened the United States on an equal, regulated basis to the non-European world, bringing a third massive wave of international migration, for the first time in American history overwhelmingly from outside Europe. Now America's immigrants come from Asia, Latin America, and elsewhere in the developing world. The epic historical processes that transformed Europe in the nineteenth and early twentieth centuries are taking place throughout the globe. Today's immigrants are in search of security and opportunity, as were the immigrants of the past. For at least three reasons, however, the trajectories of their histories may be different. First, a significant number of today's immigrants have entered the country illegally, and thus their position is insecure. Second, today's immigrants are largely non-white. Race has formed a principal line of fragmentation within American society, and, as such, it threads its way insistently throughout the story of immigration. Race separated the experiences of voluntary immigrants in the distant past, for such minority immigrant peoples as the Mexicans, Chinese, and Japanese were perceived as inferior, menacing, and inassimilable, and they suffered significant political, economic, and social discrimination. Third, the opportunity structure of American society has greatly changed in recent decades, with possible negative consequences. Contemporary immigrants come to an increasingly de-industrialized America, where there are fewer well-paying, secure factory jobs in mass production industries of the sort that once helped propel past immigrants into the middle class.

Lower-paid, less stable service, health care, light manufacturing, and information-processing jobs make up a relatively large sector of the workforce. In contrast to the earlier century of immigration when America was a rising economic giant, the U.S. economy is being severely challenged to maintain its competitive advantage by the European Union and such emerging industrial giants as China, India, and Brazil. American workers are often competing with lower-wage workers, and American businesses and industries with more efficient as well as lower-cost operations abroad. The symbolic representations of today's immigrants reflect these changes. They consist of the Chinese family selling ethnic fast food at the local shopping mall, the veiled Somali woman who cleans guestrooms at the Holiday Inn, the Jamaican nurse, the Mexican landscape gardener, and the South Asian computer repairman. Although the actual socioeconomic profile of today's immigrants is far more complicated, these immigrants nonetheless appear to fit more tentatively into American society than past immigrants.

A source of debate and conflict

Mass immigration has been a source of division among Americans, but the intensity of that division waxes and wanes over time. Because so many Americans have their origins somewhere else, they might applaud the melting pot society that immigration assisted in creating. Yet amid a vast tide of newcomers, they have been deeply divided on whether mass immigration is a benign development, or a necessary one, or an evil to be eradicated. Indeed, the effects of immigration upon employment and wage scales; political alignments and the workings of government; schools and other public institutions; the language spoken in the streets, in the shops, and in government offices; public morality and crime; resource allocation and depletion; and population growth itself, all constitute ongoing points of public argument, with nativists and pluralists repeatedly squaring off against each other. Both sides display little understanding that these same issues have been debated many times before in much the same terms.

Immigration and immigrants have continually been criticized by those nativists abhorring the culturally and socially disorganizing presence of so many foreigners. Workers, native and ethnic alike, and often their labor unions lament the depressing effect on wages and living standards that (they argue) results from the entrance into the country of so many low-wage foreign workers. Immigration and immigrants have continually been defended by those pluralists valuing diversity for its own sake and as the benign essence of Americanism, or honoring the memories of their immigrant ancestors, or seeking to find a place in America for their own foreign kinfolk. They have been allied with employers, who have little concern for diversity per se, but are eager to employ cheap labor. Thus, unlikely political coalitions have historically formed around immigration. Social conservatives and labor unions, on the one hand, and democratic idealists, ethnics, and conservative capitalists, on the other, have squared off against each other continually in debates about policy and law.

The popular debate stirs a nagging, core issue, beyond perennial policy questions such as the language of instruction in the public schools or the effect of immigrants on wages and living standards, which appear and are temporarily resolved or forgotten, and then reappear when new immigrants arrive. The debate is a forum in which Americans have struggled collectively to define themselves. For one side, the core of American culture, descended through the centuries, is and must remain Anglo-American. For the other, the culture continually evolves, with a vast variety of peoples leaving their mark and the accommodation of difference itself generating creativity.

The issue ultimately is, "Who are we?" In a world in which nation-states have come to be imagined as communities providing definitions of identity for millions of unrelated, unacquainted individuals, for many that question ultimately presents the existential problem: "Who am *I*?" Such questions themselves are staples of modern life. As identities have become more fluid and diverse amid the instabilities of modernity, identity has become problematic. But such questions are overdetermined in the United States, a relatively young society, with a population continually reconfigured by massive immigrations from without and ceaseless movement within its borders. Many cannot accept the answer, "We are everyone." They do not want to consider themselves to be like those who represent, whether on the basis of visible traits like skin color or of the sound of a language they cannot understand, the antithesis of their ideal image of themselves.

So the debate continues. It is reflected in the shifting character of immigration law and policy. At first, there was little effort to regulate the flow of immigrants into the country, and only non-white people—*white* itself not closely defined—were barred from becoming naturalized citizens. Increasingly over the course of the late nineteenth and early twentieth centuries, Asians of a variety of origins were barred from entrance because of race, and some Europeans were excluded because of health, disability, political belief, criminal record, literacy, or poverty, and finally in 1921 and 1924 restricted through quotas on the basis of national origin. Then, in 1965, the gates were opened to all peoples, with limits only on the absolute numbers from each hemisphere, in part to appease a guilty national conscience made vulnerable in the midst of Cold War ideological struggles by the racism of past immigration law. Thereafter, legislation was passed to confront the controversy swirling around the vast tide of immigration, legal and illegal alike, the 1965 law produced.

Myths and realities about the reception of strangers

Disagreements over the benefits of immigration suggest that what might prompt a memory of a common or ancestral experience among tens of millions of Americans does not really serve to unite them. It is not for want of powerful, potentially unifying symbols

1. After being brought there by ferry boats from the ships that had carried them across the sea, immigrants waited in the Main Hall at Ellis Island to begin official processing by doctors and inspectors.

of immigration. Consider the Statue of Liberty, and its poetic companion, Emma Lazarus's poem *The New Colossus*, written for the statue's dedication in 1886. Both give material form to the oral traditions of millions of contemporary Americans, and provide an emotionally compelling immigration myth celebrating the redemptive powers of American democracy. It is the narrative of Lazarus's "huddled masses yearning to breathe free." They arrive poor and exhausted, or as Lazarus, the descendent of Portuguese Jewish immigrants, would have it in her unpromising characterization, as "wretched refuse." Consider, too, not far away in New York harbor, Ellis Island, the nation's largest immigrant receiving center for many decades, a site made into a powerfully evocative legend through the popularization of historical photographs and the skillful marketing tactics of those who saved it from ruin after it fell into disuse in the mid-twentieth century. Here Europeans, the vast majority of immigrants historically, were processed before their journeys to the mainland.

7

In the photographs taken at Ellis Island, most of the subjects look unprepared for their American lives, but as popular oral tradition has it they were hardworking and aspiring, and without assistance from government, aided only by family and through their own efforts to build community solidarity, they took advantage of the gift of American liberty to improve themselves. While they were less welcomed than simply admitted to the United States and they encountered many difficulties in resettling and establishing permanence, they ultimately prevailed in the struggle for material security and prosperity. In the process, it is said, they became Americans, with a powerful feeling of belonging to their new country.

The myth may contain some truth for understanding the majority of white European immigrants and their ethnic descendents. It does not help us to understand those not considered white, for their naturalization was hindered at the very birth of the country by legislation that limited citizenship to white people, though that principle was unevenly applied over time, and their immigration was proscribed in later decades. Chinese immigration was largely halted by law after 1882, and law and policy thereafter badly disrupted Chinese American culture by hindering family formation and withholding opportunity. Angel Island in San Francisco harbor, where Chinese and other Asian immigrants disembarked and were subject to all manner of official harassment, has symbolic implications very different from those of Ellis Island.

Nor might it assist us in understanding the lives of those many thousands of Mexicans or Filipinos who were coerced into returning to their countries during the Great Depression of the 1930s because local and state governments preferred to support the white unemployed, or of the 110,000 Japanese, most of the Japanese American population and 62 percent of them American citizens, forced into internment camps during World War II. Though all of these non-European groups found an integral place in American society after 1945, their struggles to do so were especially intense because of racism.

2. Three official notices displayed and taped to a building: Air Raid Shelter Notice and Japanese Exclusion [from the Pacific coastal region] and Internment Notices. Long-standing racial animosities and panic over the prospects of Japanese attacks on the American mainland facilitated by spying by Japanese Americans led to incarceration of 120,000 people, most of them citizens, during World War II.

Yet even for the massive number of Europeans, the story of American immigration is much more complex than any self-congratulatory, patriotic narrative would have us believe. While European immigrants were rarely greeted with open arms by immigration officials and by Americans in general when they arrived, they were nonetheless, often grudgingly, regarded as *white* in a society where color was already a marker of status. However, they were often conceived by Americans as if they were members of different races, because *race* in this historical context often implied not color, but what we today might call *nationality*. Used in this way, *race* often carried the idea that peoples who did not look much different from Americans might nonetheless bear

9

inner, ineradicable, mostly negative traits to which culture and small points of physiognomy were a clue.

The processing of immigrants at the point of disembarkation was much less formal for everyone before the early twentieth century, but at that time it became impersonal and bureaucratic, and worked with assembly-line precision. In light of the many millions of people to be processed in the late nineteenth and early twentieth centuries, it is difficult to imagine it could have been done differently. But beyond the situation itself, immigration, whether that of the cruelly treated immigrant Chinese at Angel Island or the impersonally processed Italian at Ellis Island, was an especially important point on which emerging conceptions of American national interest were focused. The American state was in part coming to maturity through exercising sovereignty at its borders, separating the acceptable from the undesirable entrant, and its efforts combined the essential challenges of recruiting a labor force, protecting public safety, and rejecting those deemed incapable of supporting themselves, all rendered through the prism of prejudices generated by ideas of race and nationality. Approximately 99 percent of the European immigrants of the late nineteenth and early twentieth centuries came through the process successfully, while the other 1 percent was turned away on a variety of political, social, and physical criteria. In contrast, one-quarter of the Chinese were excluded.

For all immigrants, scrutiny at the border was an anxiety-producing encounter, but for most Europeans it amounted to momentary discomfort. Their labor was needed. The masses of working people, especially those from Ireland and southern and eastern Europe, were not believed to be as good material for citizenship and civilized living as the white, native-born Americans of Anglo-American stock, who commanded the public and private institutions of the country and sought to set the tone of its manners and morals. But these immigrants were tentatively, though hardly universally, regarded as capable of self-improvement and becoming partners in national progress.

The European immigrants took the country, with its abiding inequalities, as they found it, which proved challenge enough. Their greatest challenge lay in learning enough of the rules and habits of the new society to be able to make a living and, if they decided to stay in the United States (and many never intended to), attain material security. While a society profoundly embedded with racial privileges and disabilities, America was also from the start a class society. Large numbers of the first white inhabitants in the cash-crop producing southern colonies were bonded laborers, working out a term of service under conditions somewhere between slavery and freedom. Deep inequalities of power and wealth among America's people have been the rule. Though it made the path smoother, to be white has hardly been a guarantee of adequate means, let alone respectability or civic equality.

The many millions of European immigrants could become citizens, and they then could vote and enjoy the other guarantees of citizenship, such as security in the ownership and transfer of property—if they were fortunate enough to have any. This was, of course, a relative achievement. Native Americans and, after Emancipation following the Civil War, African Americans were hardly secure in their citizenship, and the racialized non-white immigrants, though arriving voluntarily, suffered formal and informal disabilities that might leave them with no secure framework of citizenship. All these non-white peoples might suffer severe discrimination in earning a livelihood, even a poorly paid one. The racialization of the European groups led to legislation to curb their numbers, but never to bar their entry.

Although European immigrants may not have faced comprehensive social and political discrimination, in material terms they generally began their American careers near the bottom of society, not far above the domestic racial groups and the racialized voluntary immigrants. European immigrants toiled on their small farms, which were rendered increasingly obsolete by commercialized agriculture. They worked in massive, regimented, and frequently unsafe factories or in small sweatshops in tenement rooms, which doubled as the living quarters of a family. They extracted coal in accident-plagued mines that supplied the energy for the American industrial revolution. In cold or heat, they dug ditches, or laid down subway tracks in the great metropolises. Some did well, but most of them never became affluent. The collective power of labor unions and of the ethnic vote increasingly counted as much in their advancement as did the work ethic of the individual.

American history has been comprised of many types of struggles to realize the promise of America held out in politicians' speeches and in the patriotic books read in the public schools, but often mocked in daily life. In the histories of American electoral politics, the labor movement and various race-based civil rights movements, a number of these struggles came together in ways that helped to transform the United States in the twentieth century into a more just society. Often amid bitter conflict, American diversity and American justice have advanced alongside one another.

This book is composed of three parts. Part I outlines in three chronological chapters the evolution of American law and policy regarding immigration and citizenship. It presents the ideologies and state actions responsible for the cycles of exclusion and inclusion framing the history of voluntary immigration, in all its national and social variety. Part II analyzes the history of population movements from multiple homeland locations to the United States, and the experience of geographical resettlement within America, an experience framed by the pursuit of economic opportunity and cultural stability in which the immigrants' own aspirations, strategies, and activities have played a crucial role.

Part III lays out the case for assimilation as a common historical framework for the history of immigrant lives and the integration of American ethnic groups, and discusses the shaping of the American mainstream around diversity. In doing so, it creates a framework for evaluating the possibilities for the future of American diversity.

Part I

The law of immigration and the legal construction of citizenship

Over centuries the modernization of economies and societies, and the growth of technologies and transportation and communication, have led to constant movement among many of the world's peoples, whose displacement in their homelands has encouraged them to seek opportunities far beyond them. But people on the move have not been able to migrate around the world with complete freedom and resettle wherever they wish. Societies desiring immigrant labor have sought nonetheless to control the flow of people across their borders, especially when that flow seemed to have reached proportions believed likely to create disorder. Relatedly, all migratory peoples have not been equally welcomed in the same society. Reactions to immigrants based on race and nationality have commonly led to calls for limiting numbers or for exclusion.

In America, law and policy have been mobilized to structure and at times limit immigration. The ideological sources of this evolution have been complex. Persisting alongside the recognition of the need for immigrant labor has been nativism, which has manifested itself in the fear and dislike of foreigners and the perception that immigration destabilizes politics, society, and culture. Popular nativist feeling has always possessed an emotional, bigoted component that invites political leaders to seek gain in recognizing and exploiting the passions of the electorate.

But nativism need not always be racist or mean-spirited; those who want the state to limit immigration and access to citizenship may have little against immigrants, and instead may be concerned about the welfare of the nation's established residents. The more benign formulations of nativism shade off into plausible arguments for restricting immigration to serve American national interests. As long as national sovereignty over borders is recognized as the right of states, and states conceive of it as their duty to serve the interests of their people, immigration policy remains a legitimate government prerogative.

As law structures immigration, it structures the composition of societies. In doing so, it shapes the imaginations of peoples within them in ways that are often not completely admitted to consciousness. By barring some people from entrance or from naturalization, while admitting others and paving the way for their citizenship, laws reproduce populations after what becomes an image of what the national stock is supposed to be. The law conditions people to regard membership in the nation as intended for some and less so, or not at all, for others.

In the American context, there has always been discontent with large-scale immigration, whether manifested in nativism or in thoughtful calls for regulation or restriction. American history has witnessed cycles of open borders, followed by the movement for state action to seal off those borders. Over time, parochial, exclusivist visions of the American people have competed with eclectic, cosmopolitan visions welcoming a broad array of peoples in large numbers. In the process of explaining themselves and fighting for adherents in the court of public opinion, both visions have struggled, as they continue to do in the present, to define national interests and national identity.

Chapter 1

Unregulated immigration and its opponents from Colonial America to the mid-nineteenth century

On the eve of its war for independence, colonial British North America had more than a century of experience of voluntary immigration. The British Crown had loosely regulated entrance of non-British subjects and made their right of residence and ultimately their naturalization subject to few restrictions, because it was eager to recruit labor. Regulatory policies were applied only sporadically. Pockets of Germans, Swedes, Finns, and Irish as well as Dutch (remaining after the British defeated the Netherlands in war and took control of New York) lived more or less as equals with the majority, who were English, Irish, and Scots.

As it evolved in law and in most places in reality, the inclusive qualities of colonial white society, in sharp contrast to the enslavement of Africans, systematic repression of the small population of free blacks, and the conquest of the Indians, did not always sit well with British residents, some of whom found immigrants from other nations undesirable and feared cultural inundation. An illustrious father of American nationhood, Benjamin Franklin, sharply reacted to the fact that his own Pennsylvania, the most diverse of the thirteen colonies, was one-third German. He expressed contempt for these Germans in 1753, stating, "[The immigrants] . . . are generally of the most ignorant stupid sort of their own nation. . . . Their own clergy have little influence over the people.... Not being used to liberty, they know not how to make a modest use of it." He complained that they refused to learn English, and that the colonial legislature eventually must translate its proceedings so that the delegates could understand one another. But officials in London and resident colonial governors blocked efforts to control immigration. Franklin and others learned that protests were futile in light of what would abide for the next 150 years as the principal rationale for a liberal immigration policy: a land rich in resources needed cheap labor to fulfill its seemingly limitless potential.

When the newly created United States addressed the question of immigration and citizenship during its first decade, it was no less generous toward white voluntary immigrants, though the discussion in Congress was pervaded by some of the same anxieties that had animated Franklin's concerns. Added to anxieties about the immigrants' capacity for citizenship were fears about foreign conspiracies by European powers aimed at bringing down the new American republic, because it might become a model of liberty for their own restive populations. Whether variously phrased in terms of religious or political subversion or terrorism, this fear would long abide in nativist thought.

Actions in Congress did not focus on immigration as such. It was more or less assumed that borders were open to all Europeans wishing to take advantage of the opening of a new country. The most important early law that addressed immigration did so only indirectly and related instead to the process of naturalization. It rested partly on the assumption that without a path to citizenship, and hence a way of attaining secure legal residence and protecting acquired property, few would consider permanent residence. Beyond this for the first eighty-five years of nationhood, the government in Washington did little directly regarding immigration. It regarded its role as limited to counting the number of immigrants entering the country and regulating the transatlantic commerce in immigrants in order to contain epidemic disease and to protect passengers from mistreatment.

The Naturalization Law of 1795 embodied a consensus in Congress on the terms of citizenship. In its basic conception of the process of becoming a citizen and of the exclusive nature of American loyalty, it would govern understandings throughout the country's history into the present. (Only in recent decades has dual citizenship, which was rejected in 1795, been accepted in the United States, as it is increasingly throughout the world.) The act stated that after five years of living in the United States, foreign residents could become citizens if (1) they had given notice two years earlier of the intention to be naturalized; (2) swore to have completed the period of legal residence; (3) foreswore other and former allegiances, renounced all foreign titles, and took an oath of loyalty; and (4) satisfied a court that they were of good character, believed in the principles of the American Constitution, and were disposed to make positive contributions to the community.

The law was only applicable to "free-born white persons," among whom nationals of countries at war with the United States were barred. Aside from its racism, which was not recognized as a moral or political problem by the Congress that passed it, in advancing belief rather than birth as the principal criteria for citizenship and its rejection of ranks and orders differentiating citizens, the law was one of the most generous of its time. Within a federal system of governance, ambiguity remained about the exact powers of the national and state governments in naturalization. This tension was removed after the American Civil War with the passage of the Fourteenth and Fifteenth Amendments to the Constitution that, in efforts to protect the civil and political rights of the newly emancipated African Americans and grant them formal citizenship, established the control of the national government. The Fourteenth Amendment created birthright citizenship as the American standard. If one were born in the United States, one was a citizen. In establishing this standard, the amendment would later create a legal situation, deeply resented by nativists, in which the American-born children of peoples, such as the Chinese or Japanese, whose immigration was tightly controlled or eventually banned, and who were originally barred by the 1795 law from becoming citizens, were nonetheless themselves American citizens. The same standard applies, equally controversially, to the American-born children of contemporary unauthorized immigrants.

Anxieties about the capacities of non-British immigrant populations for citizenship threatened in the 1840s and 1850s to erupt into a successful campaign to change the approach to naturalization. Though the years after the end of the War of 1812 witnessed a steady growth of immigration, with 751,000 people entering the country between 1820 and 1840, it was not until the European agricultural crisis of the 1840s and 1850s that immigration and its consequences gave rise to reactive nativist politics. From 1840 to 1860 more than four million individuals immigrated. The greatest cause for concern among Americans was the arrival of poor peasants and artisans, especially from Ireland and the German states, many of whom were Roman Catholic. Many Americans in the Northeast and newly emerging states of the Midwest thought their rapidly growing numbers threatened wage scales and Anglo-American Protestant cultural authority, and, as these immigrants became citizens, negatively impacted partisan alignments in elections. Some Americans believed the inhabitants of Europe's alms houses were being forced to emigrate. Their passage was thought to be paid by landlords wishing to clear them off the land to make way for commercialized agriculture and by government officials who did not want to provide public charity. The immigrants were said to be assured that they could resume lives of dependency in America's tax-funded poor houses. (This type of assisted immigration, which is associated with victims of crop failures, such as the 1840s potato famines, actually sent the displaced peasants of England, Scotland, and Ireland mostly to the British Empire locations of Canada and Australia, not the United States.)

Nativist organizations formed first among urban Anglo-American Protestant working men, and called for the suppression of mass immigration and the seemingly effortless path to citizenship. These fears were larger than anxieties about economic competition, and eventually spread beyond the working class members of nativist lodges. Part of the cultural inheritance of Anglo-America from its foundation in Reformation-era Britain was a pervasive hostility to Roman Catholicism and a fear of Vatican-directed conspiracies aimed at spreading Catholicism. Related fears of the subversive potential of enemy aliens in wartime had been partly responsible for the passage of the Alien Enemies Act of 1798, which enabled the national government to apprehend and deport aliens from countries hostile to the United States. These fears were partly stoked by the triumphalist oratory of an increasingly confident Roman Catholic hierarchy in cities like New York, which spoke from the pulpit about converting Protestant America to "true" Christianity.

Under the 1795 law immigrants petitioning for citizenship had to renounce foreign "potentates," a code word intended to include the pope as well secular monarchs, but nativists had no confidence that this would protect the United States. Many Anglo-Americans conceived of the Catholic immigrant, especially the Irish, as no better than tools of their priests. If priests directed them to be agents of the Church, there was no doubt among nativists that their sworn testimony at citizenship hearings would be a fraud, especially if the judge before whom the immigrant appeared was a Democrat, the party that profited most from German and Irish votes.

Yet ending or lessening immigration did not become a part of the national agenda. Briefly a national third party, the American

Party, was formed to advance the nativist cause in national elections in 1852 and 1856, but it rendered a version of the nativist agenda that was a disappointment to the movement's radicals. Its platform revisited the congressional debates of the 1790s, in which the precise number of years of residence in the United States deemed necessary to be born again as the citizen of a democratic republic was a principal matter for concern. Five years seemed completely off the mark for Americans contemplating thousands of impoverished Irish peasants they now saw in the streets. Thus, the party's platform rendered its anti-Catholic, anti-immigrant ideology in one promise: if elected it would extend the time required for naturalization to twenty-one years, the period from birth a native-born male usually had to wait until allowed to vote. The immigrant, in effect, had to be born and mature again.

The American Party at the national level was led by respectable, if highly opportunistic men, conservative by temperament and ideology. They had no intention of unleashing fanaticism. They knew immigrant workers and farmers were essential to American prosperity and power. Party leadership opted not to reform immigration policy, but to reform the immigrants themselves: with the passage of time they would be exposed to American life and become Americans. While vicious stereotypes about Germans and especially the Irish circulated widely, neither group was racialized to the extent that thoughtful people believed that inherent traits made them forever inadequate candidates for the blessings of American liberty.

Nativist politics declined rapidly with the crisis of the American union that led to a long, bloody Civil War (1861–65), in which immigrants and natives fought together, North and South alike, in the same armies, and which thus eventuated in a sense of unity across ethnic lines. But the older themes of nativism—subversion, loss of Anglo-American Protestant cultural authority, incapacity of peoples beyond the Anglo-American core for self-government, insecurity about wage scales, and the like—would never disappear, and they would inform larger efforts to begin to regulate immigration after 1865. Legislation passed between 1864 and 1917 barred from entering the United States: laborers who had signed contracts of employment abroad (1864, 1885) in fear of the effect on wage scales of contracts negotiated with workers completely ignorant of American conditions; convicts and prostitutes (1875); paupers, beggars, and people with tuberculosis, epileptics, the mentally ill, the developmentally disabled, and others chronically ill or physically impaired (1882, 1903) who might become public responsibilities; and illiterates (1917). In 1906, those without command of English were barred from naturalization. Some of these measures were a plausible response to problems of public health and safety. Under such laws, only about 1 percent of those Europeans arriving as immigrants at American ports were actually denied admission and sent back to their homelands.

But these seemingly plausible criteria depended for thoughtful implementation on fine distinctions and humane judgment. Although it was never absent completely, the massive bureaucratic machinery that developed over the decades to enforce immigration law was not geared to flexibility. On such questions as what degree of physical impairment left one unable to support oneself, enforcement tended to be overly cautious. Under any circumstance, many immigrants with such impairments came with support networks of friends and family awaiting them, and were not likely to turn up in the poor house. It was hardly true, in addition, that knowledge of English, let alone literacy, was necessary for the tasks that confronted ordinary immigrants. Inspectors often imagined that a woman immigrating alone who could not demonstrate ties to an American support network would inevitably fall into prostitution.

Increasingly, too, categorizing peoples was conceived through the prism of race, which overwhelmed such particularized physical, gender, mental, cognitive, political, and moral distinctions, and established what for many Americans was the most efficient, convincing way to determine who might be an American. Under the impact of racial thinking, *laissez faire* in immigration and naturalization declined, and the state's role would come to assume mammoth proportions.

Chapter 2
Regulation and exclusion

Anti-Chinese agitation

The path to regulation and exclusion began in the extraordinary melting pot that was California, newly admitted to the United States after it was seized from Mexico in the Mexican-American War (1846–48). Isolated though it was from the major transatlantic shipping lanes and without rail links to the eastern seaboard until 1868, at the time of the 1840s Gold Rush California had nonetheless attracted thousands of Americans and Europeans, Chinese, and South American immigrants, whose numbers added to the small populations of Native Americans and original Spanish and Mexican settlers.

The Chinese provided valued labor in the gold mines, on farms that provisioned the miners, and ultimately in the construction of the railroad line that would connect the West and East coasts. But in the 1870s, as California settled into a post-boom economy and confronted a severe economic depression, white workers felt their living standards were threatened by the low wages acceptable to many Chinese. A movement, inspired by a combination of economic insecurity, racial hostility, and political opportunism, took form to end Chinese immigration and force the Chinese to re-emigrate. While anti-Chinese politics had some eastern support, its epicenter would long reside in California. Its principal spokesman was Irish-born

3. **Alongside Mexicans, Irish, Americans, and others, Chinese laborers were a significant part of the workforce that constructed and maintained the first railroads of the American Far West.**

Denis Kearney, founder of the Workingmen's Party, under whose leadership the party did well in local and state elections. A powerful orator, Kearney ended every address with his signature message: "And whatever happens, the Chinese must go!"

Political representatives of the white working class, commonly themselves the product of some recent immigration like Kearney, would be prominent in developing arguments against immigration in the service of defending the welfare of the ordinary American. Not all were demagogues, to be sure, for arguments that a continual inrush of cheap labor might have a downward effect on wage scales were plausible. But when fused with hatred for the *Other*, the ugly

AT FRISCO.

"See here, me Chinee Haythun, I'm wan of the Committee of National Safety; and bringing to me moind the words of George O'Washington and Dan'l O'Webster in regarrd to Furrin Inflooince, ye must go. D'ye understand? Ye must go!"

4. The cartoonist seeks to capture the irony of an immigrant, dressed in typical Irish peasant garb and speaking with an Irish brogue, ordering a Chinese immigrant to leave the United States in the name of two famous American statesmen, George Washington and Daniel Webster.

face of class politics was racist. Evidence of such racism lay most evidently in the fact that neither Kearney nor the California labor unions advocated a class-based movement founded on the organization of all workers, whatever their nativity or race.

Throughout California, the anti-Chinese movement often engaged in violence and terror. The Chinese were an isolated, relatively small population. China lacked a government strong enough for effective diplomatic protests against such outrages. It was easy to gang up on the Chinese and convenient during election campaigns for opportunistic politicians to champion the racist white majority. But there were limits to Kearney's influence. He was not successful in convincing workers outside California that the Chinese were a real threat to them. In California itself union leaders eventually concluded that Kearney's agenda was too narrow to benefit their white constituents, and they resented his power. But Kearney did succeed in impressing Washington politicians with the influence he had attained by fusing race and immigration. The call for banning the Chinese gained widespread support, including among other racial minorities. African American newspapers, for example, denounced Chinese immigration as a threat to the precarious economic status of black workers. Congress responded, giving California's white population what the most vocal and violent within it desired: an end to most Chinese immigration; hence, the prospect the Chinese would eventually disappear. In 1882 Congress passed the Chinese Exclusion Act, which was periodically renewed until made permanent in 1904. The law was not repealed until the Magnuson Act of 1943, when China and the United States were allies in the struggle against Japan, and Chinese exclusion, an effective point in Japanese propaganda, had become a national embarrassment.

Chinese exclusion and subsequent efforts began the evolution of American immigration law and policy, as the historian Mae Ngai observes, into an engine "for massive racial engineering" that sought to use state power to define the demographic and cultural character of the nation. A force accelerating the process was the particular nature of Chinese exclusion, as Congress crafted it. The law did not bar *all* Chinese immigration, only Chinese laborers. Merchants, students, the immediate family of American-born Chinese citizens, and Chinese American citizens returning from abroad were not barred.

The problem for enforcement was sorting out those barred from those eligible for admission. The effort was often carried out with a ham-fisted brutality or cold formality, especially at the Angel Island immigration station in San Francisco harbor, where the large majority of Chinese arrivals was processed. The presumption of government immigration agents was that all Chinese seeking entrance were lying about their status. To their minds, women arriving at Angel Island were not the wives or daughters of legal residents they claimed to be, but prostitutes imported to work in the brothels catering to whites and the large Chinese bachelor population. The elaborate documentation and close interrogation stood in sharp contrast to the perfunctory questioning of most Europeans seeking entrance.

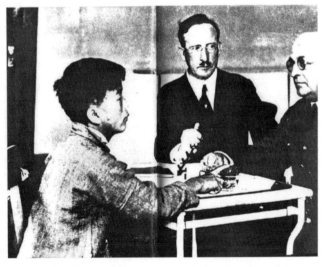

5. Angel Island interrogations were considerably more formal than those brief encounters between European immigrants and inspectors at Ellis Island. Asian immigrants usually faced one or more inspectors and a stenographer. A government interpreter translated. Questions and answers were typed out and placed in the file of applicants seeking admission.

Chinese sought to evade the law by claiming false family relationships through legally resident sponsors, or they attempted to enter the country illegally by crossing its northern or southern land-borders at a time when they were largely unpatrolled. Chinese American citizens occasionally challenged the operations of the law in court and won some notable victories. One way or another, within a decade of the Chinese Exclusion Act, the government was facing a well-publicized challenge, and it was often unsuccessful in the contest. The number of Chinese testing the law was never significant enough to be a true threat to state power, as opposed to an annoyance, but sensationalistic press coverage created panic in the general public, and federal officials and enforcement officers felt their authority was compromised and reacted aggressively.

The growth of national government activity and power

Frustrated efforts to enforce Chinese exclusion joined other sources of immigration-related anxiety: growing racial consciousness among the white majority based on contemporary science and popular attitudes; increasing concern, with a resurgence of mass European immigration, about the need for more effective regulation of immigration, borders, and citizenship processes; imperial conquest; and large numbers of mobile, U.S.-bound non-white people from Asia, the Pacific, and the Caribbean. Immigration policy moved from openness to gatekeeping, though the precise application of policies continued to depend on the origin of the immigrants.

The 1891 Immigration Act was an unambiguous statement of centralized power. It formally assigned responsibility for the assessment of people seeking entrance to the national government. Congress established the office of Superintendent of Immigration within the Treasury Department to oversee all immigration inspection, including new medical and intelligence testing, such as took place at Angel Island and Ellis Island. A bureaucracy, large for its time, took shape around processing at entrance ports and, under the jurisdiction of the Customs Service, enforcing border security along the northern and southern borders, where energies were devoted principally to rooting out small numbers of illegal Chinese entrants and the shadowy criminal enterprises that smuggled them across the Canadian and Mexican borders.

On the heels of the Chinese precedent, racially inspired proscriptions increased. Additional discriminatory responses to Asian immigration led ultimately to the exclusion of half the world's population. In 1907, during a decade in which the Japanese immigrant population tripled in the mainland United States from 24,000 to 72,000, quotas, rather than a policy of exclusion, would be applied to Japanese laborers in response to protests, especially in California. Japanese were considered less a threat to wage scales than to the monopoly of white people on prime agricultural land, for they were successful in acquiring a foothold in fruit and vegetable farming. But like the Chinese, they were deemed inassimilable. Having just won a war against Russia, however, Japan was an emerging world power, so rather than unilateral action, as had been the case with the Chinese, a quota system was negotiated between President Theodore Roosevelt and the Japanese government. Under the terms of the so-called Gentlemen's Agreement, Japanese immigration to the American mainland fell in the next decade by a third. (The recently annexed U.S. possession of Hawaii, which desperately needed Japanese sugar plantation labor, was excluded from the agreement.) Immigrants from Korea, then under Japanese control, were also limited.

Prompted by the ongoing controversy over Japanese landholding, in 1913, California and eight other western states as well as Florida took action against all landholding by aliens ineligible for citizenship. The Supreme Court declared such laws constitutional.

Because many Japanese immigrants had children born in the United States, they circumvented the law by registering their property in the names of their children. The frustrated efforts at piecemeal proscription of Asian immigration and citizenship ended in 1917, when Congress passed legislation declaring all of Asia, exclusive of the Philippines, a U.S. possession after the Spanish-American War, "the barred Asiatic zone," from which immigration must cease completely.

In this racialized climate of opinion and state action, confrontations about who was white inevitably arose when those barred from citizenship under the 1795 Naturalization Law contested their status. In the late nineteenth century, lower courts and state legislatures actually were confused about which groups fit into the category of "white persons eligible for citizenship." The federal courts sorted the matter out, though hardly on consistent intellectual grounds. Judges never resolved whether the recorded history of the evolution of peoples, or contemporary racial science, with its increasingly elaborate categories of classification of peoples, or popular prejudices would govern the crucial question of who was white. They did rule that Japanese, South Asians, Burmese, Malaysians, Thais, and Koreans were not white, while Syrians and Armenians, whom the United States Census in 1910 had actually classified as "Asiatics," were white. The birthright citizenship of the American-born children of aliens ineligible for citizenship was nonetheless affirmed.

Federal courts also addressed the racial status of Mexicans, who originally became part of the American nation after the annexation of southwestern territory conquered in the Mexican-American War. Later the numbers of Mexicans tripled between 1910 and 1920 to 652,000 residents, as a consequence of political instability and economic modernization in Mexico. After northern Mexico was annexed into the United States in the early 1850s, Mexicans were made citizens, and thus implicitly declared white persons. By a consensual fiction, Mexican lineage was declared

European, via Spain, and the Indian ancestry of Mexicans laid aside. This had served the purpose of securing the citizenship status, and hence loyalty, of numerous large landowners, especially in California. Some were Spanish in origin, but many were Mexican or descendents of Mexican and American intermarriages. A federal district court in 1897 affirmed the citizenship, and hence the whiteness, of Mexicans for purposes of citizenship.

On the popular level, however, Mexican whiteness was contested. The new immigrants were widely seen as uneducated, dirty, diseased, criminal, and lazy. Political agitation to drop them from the citizenship list failed, but in the 1920s the federal government worked to impede their entrance by increasing a head tax on Mexicans entering the country and by denying visas on the grounds that they were inassimilable and would become dependent on public assistance. During the Great Depression, large numbers of Mexicans, citizens and aliens alike, were encouraged, often to the point of coercion and with the active cooperation of diplomatic officials of the Mexican government in western cities, to leave the country. The same program of massive deportations and repatriations also befell Filipinos, who worked extensively in West Coast agriculture and canneries. Another group subject to strong racist pressures, their entrance into the country had been secured, in contrast to other Asian groups, when their homeland became an American possession. (They too, however, were barred from citizenship.) During World War II, the policy toward Mexicans was reversed, because of the shortage of agricultural labor and cannery workers. A bilateral agreement with Mexico established the *Bracero* (Spanish: day-laborer or field hand) program, which facilitated the recruitment of cheap agricultural labor through temporary work permits.

Legislators, judges, and immigration officials increasingly sorted out peoples by their presumed suitability to be Americans, as opposed to their desire to work. In consequence, Congress and the courts were faced with an endless array of challenges in the name of consistency. A particularly pressing issue was the relationships among citizens and aliens linked by marriage, which introduced the complexities of gender to those mounting in the name of race. Originally, American legislation on naturalization did not limit eligibility for citizenship by sex, but gradually the courts determined that a women's status was to be defined by that of the males to whom she was related. In 1855 Congress formally adopted the principle of derivative citizenship, which held that a woman's status was dependent on that of her husband or father. A woman who was not a citizen acquired citizenship when marrying an American citizen. The reverse of that situation, the status of a female citizen who married an alien ineligible for citizenship on the basis of race, was addressed in 1907, when Congress decided that she lost her citizenship when she married. Legally these women were no longer allowed to re-naturalize unless their husbands were naturalized first (as by an act of Congress targeted at an individual), furthering the link between a woman's status and her husband's. The loss of citizenship to such women led to much injustice and inconvenience, and caused bitter protests.

After the ratification of the Nineteenth Amendment to the Constitution enfranchising women and, in effect, creating a political status for them independent of men, the Cable Act of 1922 and a series of amendments to it in the ensuing decade were passed to address the situation. Thereafter, marriage by a woman who was an American citizen *at birth* to an alien no longer carried with it the loss of citizenship. For women acquiring their citizenship through marriage or by act of Congress, as was the case for women in Hawaii, Puerto Rico (an American possession since the Spanish-American War), and the Philippines, marriage or remarriage to an alien ineligible for citizenship continued to carry the penalty of denaturalization.

Such elaborate efforts to expand state power to classify people by gender, race and nationality stood in sharp contrast to most

Americans' desire for a small, relatively weak central government. The situation suggests the seriousness with which the electorate regarded immigration. However racist, arbitrary, and unjust, these efforts nonetheless touched a relatively small number of voluntary immigrants and their wives and children.

The massive wave of turn-of-the-century European immigration

On the East Coast, European immigrants continued to enter the country in enormous numbers. After the severe economic depression of the 1890s, the tide of immigrants reached unprecedented proportions. Between 1871 and 1900, 11.7 million immigrants arrived; between 1901 and 1920 alone 14.5 million did. The points of origin were changing dramatically. While in the nineteenth century, western and northern Europeans predominated, now southern, central, and eastern Europeans did. The former never stopped arriving, but the latter overwhelmed their numbers.

This change carried tremendous significance for Americans wary of unlimited immigration, and demand grew to curb European immigration. Behind this effort lay the transformation in both the popular mind and contemporary science of differences of culture and appearance into inheritable racial dispositions that made assimilation impossible.

The newer European immigrants *were* different in ways that alarmed many Americans. Many fewer were Protestants than the Germans, Scandinavians, British, Irish, and Dutch immigrants of the past. The majority were Jews, Orthodox of a variety of sorts, and Roman Catholic, whose presence activated long-standing prejudices and suspicions. The physical appearances of eastern European Jews, Slavs, and southern Italians and Greeks suggested a lack of racial kinship with Anglo-Americans, though these differences were no doubt accentuated by the ill-fitting peasant garb and poverty of most newcomers. The prominent sociologist Edward A. Ross spelled out these suspicions about racial difference and inferiority when he noted in 1914 that "the physiognomy of certain groups unmistakably proclaims inferiority of type." In every face, he noted "something wrong....There were so many sugar-loaf heads, moon faces, slit mouths, lantern jaws, and goose-bill noses that one might imagine a malicious jinn [genie] had amused himself by creating human beings in a set of skew-molds discarded by the Creator."

Another difference was the new immigrants' greater traditionalism. Even though they knew enough about the modern world to develop effective strategies for leaving their homelands and resettling thousands of miles away, the eastern, central, and southern Europeans were more anchored in traditional peasant social arrangements than their contemporaries within the continuing flow of western Europeans. It was easy to forget that sixty years earlier, the Irish and Germans especially seemed outlandish and had only gradually given evidence of being successfully integrated into American life. The perception of never being likely to assimilate was heightened, too, by the fact that many of the newer immigrants, in contrast to the more family-based, mid-nineteenth century immigration, were single males wishing to make as much money as possible quickly and return to their homelands.

Racialization of these Europeans never approached the ferocity seen in the popular response to such peoples as the Japanese or Chinese. American nativists condemned the backwardness of these European peoples as much on the basis of culture as biology. It was possible for thoughtful people, on the one hand, to urge a curtailing of their entrance as a reform in the name of saving America, and, on the other hand, to be sympathetic to the immigrants' aspirations and respectful of their work ethic and family orientation.

But there could be no doubt about the consequences of such racialized thinking: sharp quotas on the admission into the country of a large number of these more recently arrived European peoples that were enacted into law in 1921 and 1924. In expressing preference and disapproval, the intention was to discriminate. Turn-of-the-century newcomers might have been officially classified as "white," but as historians have observed, they were considered *in-between people* or *provisional white people*, and by 1920, in the minds of many long-established Americans, there were quite enough of them. Unlike the nativists of the mid-nineteenth century, the new advocates of radical change in immigration law and policy did not have much faith in reforming immigrants, but instead demanded reform of national policy.

The calls for restriction of these Europeans grew after 1890. Emerging at various levels of society, they had multiple sources, three of which stand out. First, the anti-foreignism inspired by mid-nineteenth century anti-Catholicism enjoyed resurgence in 1887 with the organization of the American Protective Association (APA), which gained adherents particularly in the rural and small town South and Middle West. The APA called for state control of Catholic sectarian schools in the belief they were havens of subversion. It claimed 2.5 million members in the mid-1890s, but this number soon declined because of rivalries among its leaders. By the time of its eclipse in the second decade of the twentieth century, the Ku Klux Klan, which was originally established in the South to impede the political and civic equality of emancipated slaves, was reconfiguring itself as a national, anti-Catholic, antisemitic, and anti-foreign as well as anti–African American organization. It became a major political force throughout the country in the 1920s.

Second, labor union leaders, such as the longtime head of the American Federation of Labor (AFL) Samuel Gompers, opposed unrestricted immigration, reflecting their members' anxieties about wage scales and the availability of work. Especially those AFL-affiliated craft unions representing skilled workers that were the heart of the labor movement in size, employer recognition, and political power held a restrictionist position. Many in such unions did not believe the newer immigrants could be organized, because of cultural differences and the aspirations of many to return to their homelands. To be sure, most of the immigrants were not skilled workers, and instead worked as factory hands and outdoor laborers in construction or extractive industries such as coal mining. This was the segment of the working class most retarded in its progress toward unionization, largely because of the difficulties of organizing an easily replaced, mobile work force with a large immigrant cohort. The fact that recent immigrants, often ignorant of the circumstances of their employment, were occasionally used as strikebreakers highlighted for American workers that the newcomers were poor material for organizations based on class solidarity.

Labor's conclusions at this point in time about limiting immigration actually broadly paralleled the thinking of industrial employers, among whom there was a growing consensus that for the time being the manufacturing economy had a supply of labor sufficient to its needs. In addition, influential industrialists like automobile manufacturer Henry Ford had become more concerned with the stability of their workforce and desirous of encouraging settled habits through Americanization programs and a variety of incentivized job and wage policies. Hence, relative to their past encouragement of high rates of immigration, the period found them more or less indifferent to the debate about immigration restriction.

Third, a respectable, intellectual bourgeois face of immigration control appeared in the Immigration Restriction League (IRL), which was organized in 1894 by a prestigious coalition of northeastern academics, national political leaders, and urban reformers. Alarmed at the growth of social problems and pervasive political corruption in the rapidly growing industrial cities, they blamed such conditions on the unchecked expansion of recent immigrant populations. Their thinking was also influenced by the emerging science of eugenics, which argued that states should take active steps to protect and improve the human genetic stock within their borders. Eugenicists advanced such measures as immigration control, sterilization of the disabled, and laws against interracial marriage.

The IRL did not publicly engage in defamatory xenophobia. Instead it offered a moderate, patriotic defense of the existing social order and republican social institutions, both of which its members believed to be anchored in Anglo-American culture. The IRL was composed of men of cultural authority and political power, such as the patrician Massachusetts Republican senator Henry Cabot Lodge; the Massachusetts Institute of Technology president Francis Amasa Walker, who had headed the U.S. Census in 1870 and 1880; and A. Lawrence Lowell, the longtime Harvard University president. The IRL's program was gradually enacted into law over the course of the next quarter century: increase in the head tax on immigrants to pay for expansion of inspection services; an expanded list of excluded classes; a literacy test; and finally, the capstone of its goals, numerical limitation.

The quota system

The path to numerical limitation, which was ultimately embodied in the 1921 and 1924 quota laws, began in 1907 with Congressional establishment of the Dillingham Commission. Charged with undertaking a comprehensive fact-finding investigation, it surveyed the entire field of contemporary immigration, and included reports on conditions in and movement from a large number of immigrant homelands in Europe and Asia. Consisting of thirty-nine volumes, the final report was issued in 1911. Based partly on the commissioners' on-site inspection of conditions at emigration ports in Russia, Germany, and southern Italy, the report dispelled long-held notions that European nations were emptying their poor houses and prisons and sending the inhabitants to the United States. It contained little explicit criticism of the immigrants, and praised their capacity for work and many sacrifices to achieve self-improvement.

But in generalizing about them, the report was nonetheless a peculiar mixture of balanced, objective sociological analysis and racialist pseudo-science. It rejected the notion, for example, that the immigrants' children were inherently stupid, in spite of widely circulated data about school failure, and it stated instead that both educational difficulties and tendencies toward juvenile delinquency were rooted in the social environment of city slums and ghettoes. It acknowledged, too, that immigrants were less likely to be criminals than were Americans. While it attributed some responsibility for miserable working conditions in many industries to immigrant workers' willingness to put up with employer abuses out of a desire to make money quickly and return home, it put more blame on employers than workers.

Both in biological and cultural terms, race pervaded the commissioners' findings, especially but not exclusively in regard to Asian immigrants. Asians were also praised for their work ethic, but exclusion was endorsed on the grounds of ineradicable differences. It treated European people through racialist frameworks. For example, the commission accepted the widespread notion that southern and northern Italians were of different races, which was said to help to explain the higher social and economic development of the north, among those whom Commissioner Henry Cabot Lodge called "Teutonic Italians." Nor did the commission necessarily embrace science when it conflicted with popular racialist notions. To study immigrant physiology and intellect, it employed the pioneering anthropologist Franz Boas, who took the opportunity to test the ideas of pseudo-scientific racialists such as the well-known writer and IRL member Madison Grant. Boas's skeptical conclusions were not consistently employed by the commission in evaluating the possibility of innate differences.

The commission's report endorsed limitations on immigration, recommending as its primary means to that end a literacy test, which was approved by Congress in 1917 over the veto of President Woodrow Wilson. It also recommended the development of a method for restriction based on numerical formulae. This recommendation, combined with the elaborate classification the commission had done sorting out groups, awaited for a time when both the public and political leadership were ready to endorse more radical solutions. That moment soon presented itself just after World War I. During the war the national government engaged in a massive propaganda campaign to inspire immigrants to enlist in the armed forces and to buy war bonds. But after the armistice, a long-standing variety of cultural, social, economic, and political concerns touching on the consequences of European immigration were then heightened by a panic about the loyalty of ethnic Americans brought about by the war; fears about domestic subversion prompted by the Bolshevik Revolution; a brief but sharp postwar recession; race riots and anti–African American pogroms in major cities; and a police labor strike in a major city, Boston, which briefly seemed to invite anarchy.

Not all these concerns could be linked directly to immigration, but together they led the public and its political representatives to a deeply apprehensive, conservative mood, and immigration control was one of its principal outlets, especially as immigration from a destitute, politically unstable postwar Europe recommenced. Ethnic organizations and the political representatives of heavily ethnic constituencies, especially in the big cities of the northeast and industrial Midwest, argued for continuing the liberal policy toward Europeans, but proved no match for the pro-limitation consensus building nationally. The title of the 1921 legislation, *Emergency Quota Act*, mirrors contemporary attitudes. The law maintained the ban on Asians and imposed for three years a quota system that limited European immigration to 3 percent per year for individual groups based on their presence in the population revealed in the 1910 federal census. It limited entrances to

41

6. Though questions about the loyalties of immigrants were raised in many local communities during World War I, the national government engaged in a vigorous campaign to enlist their support for the war effort.

350,000 a year, 45 percent from southern and eastern Europe and 55 percent from northern and western Europe, substituting unlimited entrance with what Mae Ngai calls a "hierarchy of desirability" among the Europeans instead of a complete ban.

When it was soon found that the law was not having the desired effect of limiting numbers, the more radical 1924 Johnson-Reed Act was passed. Beginning in 1927, immigration was to be limited to only 150,000 annually from the entire globe, exclusive of the Western Hemisphere, which was exempted from limitation in order to maintain good bilateral relations with neighbors and, via Canada and the Caribbean, with imperial Great Britain and in anticipation of the need for Mexican agricultural labor in the West and Southwest. Now quotas were to be apportioned on the basis of the 1890 census, before the vast bulk of the southern and eastern Europeans had arrived. Each nationality could make a claim to a proportion of the total based on 2 percent of its population in the United States in 1890. A commission was established to determine the exact numbers for the future, and it mandated a quota system that, while preserving a low absolute number of entrants, was based on the 1920 census, and thus more generous to the newer European groups. The new quotas went into effect in 1929, just as voluntary international population movements would begin a sharp decline because of the worldwide depression of the 1930s, totalitarian regimes in Europe that impeded or banned emigration, and eventually World War II.

Between Chinese exclusion in 1882 and 1930, the United States had evolved from an open immigration regime to a carefully constructed system that controlled and prioritized potential entrants, based largely on racialized conceptions of acceptability. The trend in this half-century may contradict much that Americans want to believe about themselves and have others believe about them, but it hardly made Americans uniquely illiberal. While the United States was banning the entrance of Japanese in 1907, Australia, New Zealand, South Africa, and

Canada were doing the same, and the Japanese themselves, firmly imbued with their own notions of racial superiority, banned Chinese and Korean immigration. While the United States was developing and imposing its quota system, other nations were evolving their own systems of restriction. With the exception of skilled workers, Canada would drop all immigration except that originating in France and the United Kingdom, homelands of its original European population groups. Argentina established a system of preferences based on Germany and Switzerland, while Brazil did so based on Italy, Portugal, and Spain. When Brazil had difficulties attracting Europeans, its government resorted to the recruitment of Japanese, and attempted to reconcile a need for labor and an embrace of racialist science by classifying them under a newly created category, "whites of Asia." Australia implemented a firmly "white Australia" policy, with preferences for immigrants from the United States and United Kingdom.

Behind the actions of these countries was the desire for greater racial homogeneity, which was widely understood to be the key to cultural homogeneity and national progress. Through eugenics, race increasingly became the basis of a program for improving a population and protecting its gene pool against invasion by those deemed inferior, while encouraging the reproduction and prosperity of those deemed worthy to be in the majority. When fused to a nationalistic foreign policy by the German fascist and Japanese imperial regimes, eugenics would become a basis for ruthless war making and genocide against those peoples and nations deemed inferior. Yet eugenics presented a powerful enough vision of the path to the human future that bitter adversaries, such as Japan and the United States, might nonetheless share at some fundamental level an understanding of how humanity might progress.

Chapter 3

Removing barriers and debating consequences in the mid-twentieth century

Emerging out of the conflict fought to turn back the lust for conquest of racist regimes, World War II was the beginning of a long process of rethinking American immigration and naturalization policy. Revocation of Chinese exclusion in 1943 in the name of accommodating an ally and countering Japanese propaganda was only a few years old when it became clear that the United States again had an international image problem on its hands. With the emergence in the late 1940s of the ideological rivalry between the West and the Soviet Union, the United States was already vulnerable to criticism that for all of its professions of defending freedom, its largest domestic minority, African Americans, lived without equal rights or opportunities, and that in the American South, a type of *apartheid*, enforced by state and popular violence, existed that resembled the South African racist regime. But African Americans did not have, as did those potential immigrants barred or subject to quotas, free and independent homelands whose governments might take offense at American immigration policy, and then lean toward neutralism or a pro-communist stance. The rethinking of the quota system, however, did not result solely from Cold War politics. There was also a widespread feeling, articulated by domestic ethnic leaders and organizations, that the quota system was an insult rooted in bigotry.

The movement toward immigration reform

The revision of the quota system came in fits and starts over the two decades after 1945, amid a vigorous debate about immigration. The first piece of major immigration legislation of the immediate postwar period, the McCarran-Walter Act (1952), did not abandon but rather revised the 1924 quotas. Passed over the veto of President Harry Truman, who argued the law sent a message harmful to American foreign policy, it retained the national origins framework, giving individual nations a quota equivalent to their proportion in the population recorded in the 1920 census. The law abandoned the whites-only policy for immigrant naturalization, but it assigned only 150,000 slots to the entire Eastern Hemisphere and provided little opportunity for Asians to gain access to legal immigration. As before, no limit was set for immigration from the Western Hemisphere. Within all populations, preference was given to skilled workers and the kinfolk of American citizens in the interest of family reunification. Finally, in keeping with the profound concerns over national security emerging during the early Cold War, and building on measures enacted during the tense years just before American entrance into World War II that required the registration and fingerprinting of all aliens, screening of those seeking residence in the United States was tightened.

Congress soon found itself forced to confront a new reality, the massive displacement of peoples on a scale previously unknown, which emerged dramatically in the wake of the World War. As many as 20 million displaced persons were homeless and stateless as the result of wartime destruction, changes in borders and regimes, the spread of state communism in Europe and Asia, and decolonization struggles that led to the collapse of European settler societies in Africa, Asia, and the Middle East. Approximately 1.8 million people languished in refugee camps run by the victorious Allied powers.

The moral and political stakes were enormous for the United States. If the nation that emerged from the war as the world's richest and most powerful did nothing to relieve this misery, what trust could be placed in its professions of moral leadership? In the background lurked the disastrous failure of the Allies to do anything on the eve of World War II to address the vulnerability of Europe's Jews before the gathering, murderous force of German antisemitism. Charities, ethnic organizations, and voluntary refugee relief organizations staffed by professionals lobbied intensely for recognition of the refugee crisis and the ideological and humanitarian stakes involved.

Refugee policy directly challenged the limitation strategies of immigration law. The Displaced Persons Act of 1948, renewed in 1950, allowed for 250,000 visas over two years for refugees, and under these acts 450,000 displaced Europeans, including many peoples such as Italians whose nations were limited by quotas, entered the country. The European bias in the legislation was corrected in acts of Congress in 1953 and 1957 that shifted the stream of refugees from Europe to Asia. Another strategy for dealing with refugees was developed by President Dwight Eisenhower, who tactically employed presidential *parole power* (discretionary power to take unilateral action in an emergency) to confront the problems of aiding masses of displaced persons. In 1956, after the failure of the Hungarian Revolution against a pro-Soviet communist regime, parole power was used to grant visas to almost 30,000 refugee Hungarians. After the Cuban Revolution in 1959, 215,000 Cubans were admitted through the same power.

Congress challenged neither of these uses of presidential power, even though their effect was to undermine the McCarran-Walter Act. A strong consensus existed that American global leadership demanded a generous recognition of persons made homeless through the expansion of the power of the Soviet and other communist regimes. The significant confrontations of the Cold War, such as the Southeast Asian conflicts, and periods of internal instability within Cuba and other Soviet client states put pressure on the United States to absorb more refugees. Refugee resettlement would be materially aided and accelerated by generous government welfare policies, inspired by both humanitarian concerns and Cold War propaganda making, which were lacking for the rank-and-file voluntary immigrant. Those policies assisted greatly in the rapid integration of Cuban and Vietnamese refugees.

These cracks in the wall of immigration restriction further inspired the efforts of an emergent coalition of reformers and reform organizations bent on overturning the quota system after 1945. The reformers intensified the immigration debate and put the supporters of the quota system increasingly on the defensive. This coalition was composed of elements possessing disparate needs but united around a common goal of changing American policy. The coalition largely overlapped with parts of the post–New Deal Democratic Party that coalesced around a social democratic and pluralist ideology of cultural diversity and progressive welfare state development. Big city ethnics with their increasingly sophisticated lobbying and defense organizations, and the liberal Democratic politicians who represented urban ethnics were major forces urging immigration liberalization. So, too, were religious and secular humanitarian organizations dealing with refugees and engaged in charitable work in countries devastated by the war. The Catholic Church's presence in European refugee and immigration work was especially strong. Its efforts mirrored both the deep embedding of American Catholicism in ethnic America and the increasing activism of the Church in public life that grew alongside acceptance of its legitimacy as an American institution.

It was not surprising to find the lobbying groups representing industry and agribusiness involved with the forces urging liberalization, for they had always equated open immigration with cheap, docile labor. But it was surprising to find labor unions increasingly identified with the cause. Union leadership had long feared the competition of low-wage immigrant labor unreceptive to organization. But in the 1950s and early 1960s the country was so prosperous, dominating the world markets for industrial goods and possessing a rapidly expanding domestic consumer market totally in the control of American business, that a liberalization of immigration policy hardly seemed a threat to the American worker. The economy's ability to absorb labor appeared to be enormous. Many unionized ethnic workers urged backing reform on their unions. In contrast to their traditional lack of enthusiasm for an open immigration policy, African American organizations also joined the coalition calling for change. The emerging civil rights movement came to understand the quota system as an expression of bigotry akin to racism. A number of its largest constituent organizations sought strategic alliances with pro-immigration reform, white, liberal politicians to advance its own anti-racism agenda.

The coalition in favor of change benefited from the prevailing optimism of the time that stemmed from unprecedented economic expansion and superpower status. The voices of isolationism had been defeated as America embraced global responsibilities, armed with the certainty of the superiority of the American way of life over communist alternatives. At home, a spirit of unity prevailed, but one that was more inclusive than that evoked by the old Anglo-American–dominated ethos of cultural homogeneity that long inspired nativism.

In the postwar period, amid unprecedented economic and educational opportunity, tens of millions of children and grandchildren of the second great wave of European immigration took advantage of the widening socioeconomic mainstream. As the economy expanded, not only did wages and salaries increase but also employment barriers that had stood in their way fell one by one, and new sectors of the economy opened to them. They entered business and the professions in large numbers, and gained in power and influence at all levels of American society. As they did, their social institutions, such as the heavily ethnic Roman Catholic Church and American Jewish synagogues, became less exotic and more a mirror of the American identity of those belonging to them. From that perspective, the great American melting pot appeared to have done its job remarkably well. Slowly and unevenly, too, the understanding that racial integration was a necessity for American progress was taking hold, as the monumental 1954 Supreme Court decision in favor of school desegregation suggested. It was difficult to believe that immigration should be conceived as a threat to American society. Diversity itself seemed increasingly to indicate strength, if people secure in their individual communities could unify for the sake of the common welfare. Though they would never disappear, the old nativist and patriotic organizations that had once warned insistently against immigration were in rapid decline.

In this mood of optimism and liberal reformism among well-organized, articulate sectors of public opinion, reformers struggled to overturn the quota system. Their efforts culminated in 1965 in the passage of the Immigration and Nationality Act, the most important piece of postwar immigration legislation. Yet the public at large was not convinced that any change in immigration law was really desirable. While reformist legislation was being debated in May of that year, public opinion polls revealed that 58 percent to 24 percent of Americans opposed changes in the law. The opposition, which was represented in Congress by a small coalition of conservative Republicans and southern Democrats, was not nearly as organized as those who confidently called for change. The general public was apprehensive along predictable lines. People worried that the cities would again be flooded with new immigrants and social problems; that the ethnic and racial balance of the population would be upset, especially if immigration shifted from white European to non-European sources; and that American workers might face declining wage scales.

The main congressional reformers were among the leading liberal political figures of the mid-twentieth century, representing constituencies with large ethnic populations. Representative Emanuel Celler of New York City and Senator Philip Hart of Michigan, known as "the conscience of the Senate," were the authors of the final piece of legislation. The principal spokesman for the law was one of the leading social democratic figures of the second half of the twentieth century, Massachusetts Democrat Edward Kennedy, who led the effort to pass the legislation in the Senate. Kennedy dedicated his efforts to the memory of his slain brother, President John F. Kennedy, a longtime advocate of immigration reform. Kennedy (Irish) and Celler (Jewish), like strong advocates for Hart-Celler New Jersey congressman Peter Rodino (Italian) and Hawaii senator Hiram Fong (Chinese) were all associated in the public mind with ethnic backgrounds.

Kennedy charged that fears about the law's likely impact were exaggerated. Countering the claims of opponents that the intention of the law was to add as many as a million immigrants annually, he stated that instead the point was to correct a wrong embedded in the quota system and to put admissions on an equal and fair foundation. Kennedy and the other reformers did not really challenge major sources of public resistance, and thus implicitly conceded that the nation was better off without mass immigration and with its existing ethnic balance.

The 1965 law passed both houses of one of the most social democratic Congresses in history by overwhelming majorities, 76 to 18 in the Senate and 326 to 69 in the House of Representatives. The law, which took effect in 1968, changed the principle underlying admissions. It abolished national-origins quotas and removed all reference to race as a selection principle. It set annual ceilings of 170,000 entrants for the Eastern Hemisphere, with a limit of 20,000 per nation, and, in contrast to the 1920s quota laws, it set ceilings for the Western Hemisphere, defined at 120,000, with no per-country limits. Visas were to be available on a first-come, first-served basis. It created a generous ordering of preferences in the distribution of visas with seven categories of desirable qualifications: family reunification; refugee status; professionals, artists, and scientists; and skilled and unskilled workers in occupations with an insufficient labor supply. Moreover, a separate track was created for family reunification, which trumped numerical restriction as a priority in the law. The number of case-specific family reunification visas issued to the spouses, minor children, siblings, and parents of U.S. citizens was potentially unlimited.

While its inclusive principles made an empathetic statement about the cosmopolitan vision held by Democratic political leadership and liberal lobbying groups, the Immigration and Nationality Act of 1965 quickly became a textbook case of unintended consequences. Many of the assurances Kennedy, Hart, and Celler gave the public about the likely consequences of reform proved to be hollow. The situation opened a gap between the public and its leadership on immigration that grew wider over the next half-century as millions of newcomers flocked to America.

Those advancing the case for reform did so with expectations framed by the dramatic narrative of nineteenth- and early-twentieth-century European immigration. In reassuring the public that the 1965 reform law would not lead to a massive tide of immigration or to a change in the ethnic balance of the country, what Kennedy and others had in mind was that, as in the past, the principal source of immigration would lie in Europe.

The resurgence of international migration in the late twentieth century

By the early 1960s, Western Europeans were riding the crest of postwar reconstruction and growing prosperity, and had little reason to emigrate. Eastern and much of Central Europe was under repressive Soviet rule that restricted the international movement of residents. It was realistic to assume European immigration would not reach the proportions it had previously, and it was also plausible to assume it might largely be restricted in the future to modest levels of family reunification. As it turned out, however, reunification was just about played out as a goal for families separated by the earlier migrations. Over the decades, cold and hot wars, genocide, and the rise and assimilation of American-born ethnic generations had led to a decline of communications between many Europeans and their increasingly distant American kin.

In sharp contrast, as modernizing economic influences, global patterns of communication and economic exchange, and political instability spread throughout Asia, South and Central America, the Caribbean, sub-Saharan and northern Africa, and the Middle East, vast numbers of peoples outside Europe came to believe that immigration offered opportunities they could not find in their own countries. The world was on the move, especially to the United States and to Western Europe, where both guest-worker programs to recruit labor for postwar reconstruction and the processes of decolonization led to the unprecedented growth of ethnic populations. By 2005, 200 million people lived outside the land of their birth.

Generously allowing for family reunification beyond ceiling numbers, liberal American immigration policy was one of the principal inspirations for this movement of the world's peoples. Shortly after the 1965 law went into effect, its consequences were seen in a rapid rise of immigration, largely from outside Europe. Immigration totals doubled between 1965 and 1970. While from 1952 to 1970 approximately 5.8 million immigrants entered the United States, between 1971 and 1986 approximately 7.3 million did. Annual legal immigration began to surpass the massive totals of the twentieth century's first decade, reaching about 1 million in 1989, and remained at that figure throughout the prosperous 1990s. In the 1990s, 60 percent of American population growth was accounted for by immigration. During the 1980s and 1990s, 13 percent of the immigrants came from Europe and 82 percent from Asia and Latin America. The top ten sending nations, in order, were Mexico, the Philippines, Vietnam, China, Taiwan, the Dominican Republic, Korea, India, the former USSR, Jamaica, and Iran.

The third massive wave of immigration promised to remake the ethnic character of the United States. By the first decade of the twenty-first century, the descendents of white Europeans were a declining percentage of the total population: 80 percent in 1980, projected to be 53 percent by 2050. "Hispanics"—the term officially employed by the American census to describe Spanish-speakers whose origins lie in South and Central America, the Caribbean, and Mexico—were the fastest growing segment of the population and supplanted African Americans as the nation's largest minority group. Hispanics, 6.4 percent of Americans in 1980, are likely to be about 25 percent in 2050.

The social and economic effects of the third wave have been hotly debated. Urban crime and social problems associated with immigration have not nearly approached the dimensions that alarmists have assumed. A number of studies have shown convincingly that immigrants are *less likely* to commit crimes or to be incarcerated than native-born Americans. In 2000, the incarceration rate among men ages eighteen to thirty-nine, the large majority of the prison population, was five times greater for natives (3.5 percent) than for immigrants (.7 percent). In California, the state with the largest immigrant population, it was eleven times greater for the same age cohort. Other studies have revealed that urban crime actually declines with an influx of immigrants, including the relatively poor. Even if greatly exaggerated by the growing ranks of the new restrictionists, however, there are enough immigrant social problems to mock the promises of the reformers of the mid-1960s.

Economists have been engaged in a spirited debate for years about whether immigrants are taking jobs from Americans, or, in contrast, fill gaps in the workforce at every level in white- and blue-collar sectors. Data on the contribution of immigrants to the economy gathered by the Immigration Policy Center, a private research institution, have charted overwhelming evidence of the multiple ways in which immigrants are vital to prosperity, as consumers, business owners, and workers. Moreover, through the taxes they pay, immigrants also make contributions that prop up the pension and medical programs of the American welfare state. These contributions are especially crucial at a time when the native-born American population is aging, has left the workforce, does not contribute proportionately to tax revenues, and requires such programs to maintain its quality of life in retirement.

A material benefit of immigration, for example, is observed in de-industrialized cities, in which immigrants have been a source of renewal amid the exodus of both industry and jobs, and the suburbanization of more affluent, native-born residents. Immigrant entrepreneurs running small commercial businesses and factories are often attracted to the decayed inner-city neighborhoods where the cost of buying or renting property is inexpensive. In the process, they have helped to renew many of America's largest cities. "If you look at what feeds the core of many American cities, it is the arrival of the immigrant groups," explained Anna Crosslin, the president of St. Louis's International Institute in 2010. Her organization, dedicated to assisting immigrants and refugees, has charted their beneficial effects on the local economy. In St. Louis new immigrants as varied as Bosnians and Chinese have used the modest savings they arrived with and small business loans to help fill the vacuum created by the collapse of the city's old mass-production economy.

Yet public opinion is not focused on debates among economists or underlying positive trends as much as street-level perceptions of daily realities. Weakened by global competition and de-industrialization over the last four decades, the American economy has not been able to deliver either the ready access to opportunity or the security that have constituted the American Dream. Immigrants are a convenient target for resultant anxieties, frustrations, and hopelessness, especially in former one-industry factory towns and small cities that long ago saw the bulk of their jobs move to offshore destinations.

The growth of illegal immigration

The massive rise in legal immigration certainly brought unanticipated and, for many Americans, troubling consequences. But it was achieved through the processes of law and attributable to a desire for fairness, within a framework defined, if inadequately, by calculations of national interest and national sovereignty. The same could not be said of an even more difficult problem that indirectly emerged out of the 1965 law: massive flows of illegal immigration, particularly in its most dramatic form across the long, porous southern border. By the plausible policy of setting an annual ceiling of 120,000 for Western Hemisphere immigration, the 1965 law had ensured a paucity of slots for the rapidly growing population of Mexico, which has the mix of structural problems that have long accompanied urbanization, industrialization, and the commercialization of agriculture. The vast differentials in social and economic development between the two neighbors guaranteed that Mexican immigration, legal and illegal alike, across the border to the United States was certain to attain large numbers and eclipse that of any other individual group. In the 1990s it was estimated that between 500,000 and 1 million Mexicans were illegally crossing the border annually in search of work. Many of these men and women were multiple border-crossers, who regularly earned wages in the United States, went home to assist their families, and returned to the United States. An underground commerce in guiding those who wished to jump the border gave rise to criminal syndicates specializing in smuggling people. Behind this vast movement of people desperate enough for work to cross the punishing southwestern deserts was the growing dependence not only of Mexicans on America, but also of American employers on low-wage, unauthorized immigrant labor. In industries such as agriculture, landscape gardening, construction, meatpacking, garment manufacture, and in the vast array of light manufacturing endeavors this was observed first in the Southwest, then increasingly throughout the country. By the prosperous mid-1990s states with expanding job markets such as Georgia or Minnesota, which had rarely seen a Mexican immigrant before, had significantly sized communities of both legal and illegal Mexican immigrants.

The problem of illegal immigration was not new. Both Chinese exclusion and the 1924 quota law caused a rapid rise in illegal entries across the northern and southern borders, complete with an underground commerce in smuggling those attempting illegal entry. Although the United States Border Patrol was created in 1924 largely in response to the need to restrict the smuggling of liquor into the country during national Prohibition, immigration control at the nation's borders soon became a vital part of the new agency's duties. The response was tougher law enforcement not only at the borders but also throughout the nation, stricter penalties for violators, and ultimately deportations, which rose from 2,700 in 1920 to 39,000 in 1929. Yet the policy was implemented unevenly. Regulations were developed to suspend deportations and regularize the status of illegal aliens in individual cases, especially in cases of family hardship. Canadian and European illegal aliens frequently benefitted from these normalizing procedures. In contrast, Mexicans, who emerged in popular lore as the stereotypical criminal border-jumper, were dealt with through deportations, especially during the Great Depression, when the scarcity of employment led to widespread protests, including among Mexican American citizens, against Mexican migrants. In the midst of a postwar boom in southwestern agriculture, illegal immigration of Mexican laborers would spike, even in the midst of the Bracero Program. In 1954 the Eisenhower administration initiated "Operation Wetback" (referring to the short swim across the Rio Grande River that was falsely believed to be the major route into the country of these workers) under which some 1 million Mexican agricultural workers were deported.

The differences between this situation and that emerging after 1965 were the greatly increased volume of those illegally crossing the border and the heightened levels of anxiety about border security that arose with, first, the Cold War and later, the threat of international terrorism. Beginning in the mid-1970s, illegal immigration became a significant and emotional issue, especially in border areas. But it was not long before both legal and illegal immigration would merge as part of a single problem—the presence of too many foreign residents—for advocates of a new restrictionism. In the late twentieth century the nation entered its third great public immigration debate.

The resurgence of controversy and debate

Beginning in 1979, with the organization of the Federation for American Immigration Reform (FAIR), a number of neo-restrictionist organizations advocated a program that variously combined a cut in the numbers of authorized immigrants, stronger border control to check illegal immigration, and penalties for employers hiring unauthorized immigrants. This program led to a public discussion that soon echoed past immigration debates. Discussed once more were protection of living standards and wage scales, crime control, national security, and safeguarding the ethnic composition of the nation as it had stood at mid-century. Added to this was a new concern: environmental degradation that accompanied population growth, much of it now accounted for by immigration. This issue contributed to the presence of some environmentalists among the new restrictionists.

The tone of the contemporary restrictionist campaign varied greatly. It is possible to argue the matter of immigration in terms of national interests, completely independent of judgments on the character of contemporary immigrants, and a number of individuals and organizations have done so responsibly and effectively. But the old nativist arguments that judged the character of the immigrants defective for the work of both self-governance and sustaining an Anglo-American cultural core (which had long ago ceased to exist) inevitably came into play. At the fringe of the new restrictionism were radical right-wing groups, such the various factions of the Ku Klux Klan, American Nazis, and armed civilian border vigilantes, all of whom maintained that the country was at war on its southern border and employed racist imagery to assert that a vulnerable white America would succumb to invading brown hordes.

Also familiar were the forces supporting the post-1965 regime. While not defending illegal immigration, they supported the unauthorized immigrant, who they viewed, in direct contrast to the image held by many restrictionists, not as a criminal, but instead as a hard-working individual desperate for opportunity. The anti-restrictionist movement consisted of ethnic organizations, especially those representing Mexicans, who united in response to the extremity of the language they heard from the racist and nativist elements of the restriction movement. All legal immigrants have been concerned that family reunification remains a key principle of American law. Allied with ethnic organizations were church and humanitarian organizations of the type that had supported the 1965 reform law. Also, employers of immigrant labor, legal and illegal, argued that in an age of global competition, rising costs, and weakening profit margins they could not stay in business unless they took advantage of the cheapest labor they could find. In congressional hearings, a spokeswoman for the lobbying organization representing the massive California landscaping industry said frankly that the companies she represented were doomed to go out of business if they had to pay competitive wages. They were dependent on illegal immigrant labor, and they routinely broke the law.

Statements of this type impressed labor union leaders with the fact that employers were going to use illegal immigrants to depress wage scales. Segments of the labor movement, which initially displayed a traditional lack of enthusiasm for the new immigrants, began to realize the futility of expecting that recent immigrants were going to go away or be sent home, and moved to organize them at their workplaces. Thus, employers and the unions that challenged them found themselves in a tenuous alliance. Whatever direction these groups came from in defending the unauthorized immigrant, they could all point to studies that have shown the enormous contribution in taxes, economic output, and consumer expenditures made by these immigrants.

If the forces arrayed in defense of the illegal immigrant mostly looked familiar, their arguments certainly have carried the marks in two ways of an emerging globalized consciousness that fundamentally challenged the logic of national interests, on which immigration policy had long been debated. First, they argued that the global imbalance of power and wealth, by which Mexico was poor and underdeveloped and its neighbor among the richest countries in the world, required special American efforts of assistance to Mexican immigrants through, for example, a revitalized system of temporary work permits. Second, in their defense of illegal immigration, anti-restrictionists walked a fine line between humanitarian concerns and indifference to law breaking.

In embracing the former argument, they challenged the concept of national sovereignty that enabled a state to define its own interests in immigration policy. They argued for a global standard of human rights that encompassed not only the right to leave one's homeland but also the right to go elsewhere to find work, setting aside completely the issue of whether there was an intention to stay and change loyalties, which had become completely beside the point in this contention. In the late twentieth century these views gained plausibility, because national sovereignties had ceded

7. Proposed legislation to criminalize illegal immigration led to large street protests in San Francisco in the 1990s. In urging freedom for the movement of those seeking opportunity, the protesters often challenged the logic of national sovereignty that gave states exclusive control over their borders.

some ground to an emerging global economic order. The ease of international movements in a globalized market for labor led increasingly to the legal recognition in many countries, whether immigrant-sending or immigrant-receiving, of dual citizenship. Moreover, developing labor-exporting countries hoped to interest their emigrants in eventually returning home with their savings and skills. Even the United States, which had long insisted on the complete renunciation of other loyalties in its naturalization process, began in the 1970s to accept dual citizenship.

Questioning the principle of national sovereignty opened the way for inquiry into how to compute the moral calculus of gain and loss in rethinking twenty-first-century immigration policy. In the minds of anti-restrictionists, what seemed transparent to restrictionists—that unauthorized aliens were at some level criminals—was not an especially pressing matter. For anti-restrictionists, the restrictionist's "illegal immigrant" was instead an "undocumented worker" or "unauthorized immigrant," terms that referred to the fact that since 1924, one had to receive a visa to enter the United States at a counselor office outside the country. No wonder that in an increasingly polarized, bitter debate, observers perceived the two sides as arguing past one another.

Action by Congress to confront the multiple unintended consequences of the change in law and policy in 1965 did not deviate greatly from past approaches. Behind congressional responses to the gathering sense of an immigration crisis and legislative impotence in dealing with it was an alarmed, angry public. Throughout the 1980s, as the economy went into and then began tentatively to emerge from the worst recession up to that time since World War II, polling revealed overwhelming majorities for sanctions against employers hiring illegal immigrants (77 percent) and for halting all immigration when unemployment reached more than 5 percent (66 percent). These numbers remained constant throughout the decade. In 1995 American public opinion stood fifth in the world (62.3 percent) in the number of people wanting prohibition or restriction of immigration. Proof that the problem of immigration was becoming a worldwide concern is suggested by the fact that this desire was even higher in the Philippines, Taiwan, South Africa, and Poland, which were themselves also exporters of people, generally educated and skilled citizens seeking well-paying employment.

Legislation in 1978, 1986, 1990, and 1996 veered in a number of directions simultaneously, as if policymakers were overwhelmed by the moral, societal, and international complexity of the problem. Alternately legislated were: numerical limitations (while preserving family reunification); amnesty for unauthorized immigrants; penalties for employers of unauthorized immigrants; expansion of the number of visas for technical workers; and

8. Fears for national security in the wake of September 11, 2001, and hostility to the massive evasion of immigration laws on the border with Mexico, led to the building of a fence over well-traveled, unauthorized border crossings. Few believed it was a solution to the problem of illegal immigration.

greater funds for border controls and deportation measures for illegal aliens. The plausibility of seeing the problem as a law-enforcement issue seemed to grow after 9/11, when the administration of President George W. Bush militarized the southern border and erected an imposing fence across the more well-traveled border-jumping routes.

The contradictory directions of this legislation are evidence of the complexity of the problem that a world on the move has created for law makers and law enforcers. In the first decade of the twenty-first century, neither American political party was willing to directly take on the multiple policy challenges associated with immigration. Debates over public policy continued, but the political risks of moving forward, in the midst of the polarization of articulate opinion blocs and the anger of much of the general public, were rightly construed as enormous.

Part II
Emigration and immigration: from the international migrants' perspectives

International population movements appear at first glance to be composed of an inchoate mass of uprooted victims who have been driven from their homes to destinations for which they are unprepared. It is true that the spreading out of modernizing forces throughout the globe in recent centuries has indeed had disruptive consequences for ordinary people, destroying accustomed ways of life by undermining their economic and social foundations. But these same modernizing forces have created opportunities for prosperity and security, promising enough to lead many people to consider permanently changing their residence. This section is devoted to understanding immigration and resettlement from the perspectives of the people within these massive migration cohorts. It traces the processes through which people have organized long-distance migration within networks defined not simply by nation but also by family, friends, and community.

Tens of millions of individual stories are united when we consider the *purposefulness* of voluntary international migration. Voluntary migration is a choice. To be sure, it is seldom an easy choice, and it has often been made within a calculus of narrow, difficult options that carry risks and lifelong implications. To exercise this choice immigrants must be active agents, engaged in strategic planning about the use of the resources they possess that can be mobilized to accomplish movement across oceans and resettlement in new societies.

In the nineteenth and early twentieth centuries, during the classic era of European immigration to the United States, immigrants fused together social and cultural resources to expedite immigration. Such cultural characteristics of modernizing change as mass literacy, cheap mass-produced publications, and state postal systems that made possible the inexpensive exchange of letters over vast distance were key elements in acquiring the knowledge that there were alternatives in the world to the limited prospects available at home. Letters exchanged between immigrants and people in their homelands facilitated the forging of migration chains. In letters, the pioneers of an immigration flow might encourage others to follow them, and they often assisted their passage; hence chains were formed between societies. Postal exchange also facilitated sending money in the form of remittances home to the old country to help family negotiate the forces of social change. As literacy expanded and popular print culture arose to satisfy the thirst of ordinary people for reading matter, newspapers and guidebooks offered knowledge of the world.

Far from breaking down under the impact of large, disruptive modernizing transformations, family and communal relationships were key to the ways in which international migration was consciously and strategically organized by individuals in the absence of assistance by governments and elites. When fused with contemporary media of communication and exchange, personal relationships continue to be the way in which ordinary people organize long-distance movement. What the personal letter once was in facilitating the exchange of information and money among emigrants and their kin and friends, e-mail, international long-distance telephone service, texting, and global electronic banking services are in the twenty-first century.

Dissemination of knowledge of the American way of life across the face of Europe and Asia, and the links that enabled travel to the United States in the nineteenth and early twentieth centuries were products of the gradual extension of trade and transportation between continents. Today, American cultural influences pervade the imaginations of people throughout the world long before they consider immigration. A tightly knit web of communications and transportation already girdles the globe, facilitating movement of people and information everywhere.

The large social, cultural, and economic forces that have provided foundations for international migration, like the legal systems that have been developed to regulate it, can explain what has constrained and facilitated long-distance population movements. But they do not provide explanations for questions such as: Who has emigrated? Why have people chosen one local destination over another? Have they intended permanent or temporary resettlement? Answers to such questions underscore the nature of international migration as a purposeful activity. They lead us to see emigration and immigration as highly selective processes involving some people and not others. One implication is that immigrants are people of singular ambition with a strong work ethic and high aspirations to improve themselves. These are traits that lend themselves to economic and social integration, even amid the difficulties of resettling in a new society.

In thinking about international migration as a selective process, consider the fact that many millions though they may be, immigrants have not constituted a significant percentage of any society they left. Few nations in Europe sent as many people abroad as Norway, from which 677,000 emigrated between 1865 and 1915, most to America. Yet with steady population growth, based on gradual improvement of possibilities for prospering in Norway, over time the number leaving that country actually represents a declining proportion of its people. Relative to total population, the percentage of Norwegians emigrating fell from approximately 40 percent to 20 percent in those four decades. Most Norwegians stayed at home. During the great age of European emigration, the same could be said of the continent in general: only three persons per thousand emigrated, and some countries, such as France and the Netherlands, sent many fewer people abroad as emigrants than did others. In 2005, while some 200 million people throughout the world resided outside the country of their birth, a very large number in absolute terms, they were no more than 3 percent of the world's population.

Within all countries of emigration, particularized local, regional, occupational, and communal streams of movement have differentiated these relatively few individuals on the move from the vast majority who chose not to migrate. It is for this reason that attempting to know emigrants by nation alone may actually limit our understandings of them. While what is most distinctive and attention-grabbing about people in terms of their history, language, culture, and appearance seems most easily explained, in shorthand fashion, by nationality, this is not necessarily the best way to understand international population movements.

Moreover, international migrants have sought multiple destinations, not just the United States, and this also suggests the complexity of choice and planning underlying emigration. They moved within their own countries, from rural areas to towns and cities. They moved to nearby countries seasonally or permanently, as did Poles migrating to France and Germany, and Italians migrating to France, Germany, and Switzerland to work in agriculture, mines, and factories. Chinese have a long tradition of migrations in search of work and trade throughout Southeast Asia that predates their resettlement in the United States. Japanese began to migrate as contract laborers to work on Hawaiian plantations before Hawaii became an American possession in 1898. So many became permanent residents of the islands that by 1940, there were twice as many Japanese residents of Hawaii as there were living on the entire American mainland. During these same decades the Japanese were also establishing themselves, as were the Chinese, in significant numbers in Brazil and Peru, where they not only provided much-needed wage labor but also such commercial services as storekeeping in societies with a weak middle class. A century ago, Australia, Argentina, Brazil, Chile, Canada, and South Africa were attracting a wide variety of peoples from many of the same points of origin as the United States. By the late twentieth century, almost every developed or rapidly developing society, whether in North or South America, Western Europe, West Africa, the Gulf States, or Australia and New Zealand, attracted immigrants from poorer or less developed countries eager to find opportunities that were scarce in their homelands.

Immigration has not necessarily been a permanent condition for all those who leave their homelands, and this, too, helps in understanding its selectivity as a process and its purposefulness. As part of a long-range plan, or because of unemployment, nostalgia, physical illness, or failure to realize their goals, immigrants have often chosen to re-emigrate. During years (1908–23) of the highest incidence of European immigration to the United States, approximately 3 million re-emigrated. To make the picture even more complex, some of these individuals, inestimable in number, chose to return again to the United States to work, though for how long can not be known.

Movement across oceans and the transnational planning it required was facilitated by the revolutions in transportation. During the age of sailing craft, the unpleasant, unhealthy voyage of approximately at least four to six weeks across the Atlantic from Europe was an experience few wanted to repeat, though some certainly did. Seasickness and fever diseases afflicted even the heartiest individuals, and burials at sea formed traumatic memories. The great steamships significantly reduced the cost (at least for the cheapest ticket), danger, discomfort, and duration (to a week to ten days) of the journey, and, like jet aircraft today for today's migrants, made it possible to go and come with much greater facility. Increasingly the shipping lines formed agreements with the railroads that allowed individuals to be ticketed through, with guidance offered, to their inland destinations. As such individuals as construction workers, building artisans, and skilled textile workers began to integrate job markets in their homelands and in the United States, what were, in effect, seasonal, transoceanic commuting relationships became possible. In a world of air travel, such possibilities seem easier now than ever. But most immigrants have limited means. Such is the case, for example, with contemporary immigrants to the United States from the Caribbean. Transportation to their homelands is easily found, but every dollar they spend on travel is less money to support their relatively more costly lives in America, or to send to help support their families in their island homes.

The immigrants discussed in the next two chapters are not confused, rootless people who are hostages to forces beyond their control. Men and women, farmers and industrial workers, storeowners and domestic workers, adults and children, in all their variety they are less violently uprooted from familiar circumstances than self-transplanted into more promising settings. The historian John Bodnar has suggested the mentality that has typified such modern immigrants is pragmatic. Open to change, they test the world around them to see what works in responding to it, and then adopt strategies that appear likely to succeed, while acknowledging the need to continue to readjust amid constant change.

Yet this flexible, risk-taking, modern state of mind has been placed mostly in defense of traditional and conservative goals—security and stability, especially for the family, measured in terms of the improvement in housing, diet, and clothing rather than in wealth and extravagant consumption. In this sense, the typical immigrant's mentality has been that of a venturesome conservative, who employs new strategies in pursuit of recognizably traditional aspirations. Immigration and resettlement have their tragic dimensions; leaving one's homeland, familiar circumstances, and friends and family are never easy. Immigrants have often been poor in the places of resettlement, and they have done backbreaking and dangerous work. But theirs is also a story of creativity in prevailing over difficulty and of small but real gains that have increased security, prosperity, and dignity.

Chapter 4
Mass population movements and resettlement, 1820–1924

The rise of modern international migration

Large-scale, transformative social processes framed boundaries within which the age of mass international migration out of Europe occurred after 1820. These processes produced the historical context in which, within a century, the overlying historical purpose of international migration could be realized: societies with too many people and hence an excess of labor exported their surplus population to emergent societies in the Western Hemisphere and Australasia that needed labor. These receiving societies were principally the United States (35 million), Argentina (6 million), Canada (5 million), Brazil (4 million), and Australia (3.5 million), all rich in resources, especially arable land, but lacking population sufficient to develop them. In 1800, only 4 percent of Europeans were living outside Europe and Russian Siberia; in 1914, by which time about 60 million people over a century had left Europe, approximately 21 percent of Europeans were living outside the continent. The population of the United States would have been only 60 percent of the numbers achieved by 1940 without international migration. It is impossible to overestimate the extent to which that additional 40 percent contributed to making the United States the world's largest economy.

Colonialism also spread Europeans throughout the world. Some colonial powers used settler colonies, such as Algeria or Indonesia, to create opportunities for hundreds of thousands of ordinary people, while extending national power. Thus, colonial migrations might supplant voluntary immigration to other sovereign states as a way of dealing with excess population. But speaking for continental Europe as a whole, nothing matched international voluntary emigration as a process for shedding excess population. Possessing the largest empire in the world in the nineteenth century, Great Britain sent millions of military personnel, civil servants, colonial officials, and settlers to far-flung colonial destinations. Nonetheless, it had the third largest cohort of immigrants to the United States, after Germany and Italy, between 1820 and 1970.

9. **Emigrants at Bremerhaven waiting to board ship for America. Bremerhaven was the leading emigration port for Germans, the largest nineteenth-century group to immigrate to America. The port also collected people from all over central and Eastern Europe, who traveled there to find ships sailing to the United States.**

A fateful demographic transition that began in Europe and would reach the rest of the world in the twentieth century has been at the heart of the rise of modern immigration patterns. After 1750 Europe's population began a very rapid ascent, first in western Europe and then, by the mid-nineteenth century, in central, southern and eastern Europe. Much of this growth is explained by improvements in diet that were made possible, for example, by the cultivation of the potato, originally a New World crop. Until catastrophic crop failures due to a fungus infection in the 1840s in France, the Netherlands, some of the German states, the Scottish Highlands, and especially Ireland, where a million died of starvation and disease, and almost 2 million were forced to emigrate, the potato was a principal staple of peasant diets.

In addition, long before the antibiotic revolution in medical pharmacology in the mid-twentieth century, improvements in sanitation that included more potable drinking water, better waste disposal, and aseptic child-birthing brought down morality rates. Typically there was no significant expansion in the amount of arable land, so population growth placed pressure on food supplies for the peasant majority, which was engaged in a wide variety of land-owning, leasing, or renting relationships characteristic of European agriculture.

The consequences are seen in patterns of landholding. When inheritance laws and customs favored the eldest son, younger sons found themselves unable to find land at prices that provided opportunity for an independent existence. But where there was partible inheritance, with the passage of generations, many sons found themselves in possession of smaller and smaller holdings that could not sustain existence. The same situation also could be seen in leasing or renting relationships, in which expectations of generational continuity on a given piece of land were disrupted by growing numbers. Even land of no more than marginal value was for sale at escalating prices. Under the circumstances, leaving the land often seemed the only way to survive.

That was only one face of the crisis of agriculture. The growth of population and the related rise of people living in the industrial cities encouraged the commercialization of agriculture, through which the cultivation of both food and fiber, using technology and scientific cultivation, was placed on an industrial footing. Peasants were reduced to wage laborers in rural areas, and their customary rights, including long-term lease arrangements, were destroyed.

Key to the process of commercialization was the consolidation of holdings. Extensive cultivation over vast acreage created the basis for significant economies of scale and a vast potential for production and profit. The traditional patchwork pattern of small holdings, farmed by people often barely making a living for themselves, and the ancient common lands that they shared for grazing work-animals and livestock, were antithetical to capitalist agriculture. Consolidation might be accomplished by increasing rents, outright evictions, or simply declaring that after the death of the current renters, the property would be unavailable for habitation and cultivation. Thus, peasants lost their access to long-term arrangements by which they knew security, and they were reduced to wage labor in the countryside or in the city. Landlords easily grasped the logic of ending small leasing and rental arrangements, increasing rents to new, commercially minded tenants, consolidating arable lands, and enclosing the common fields for use in the future of commercial herds.

Some large rural economies outside Europe experienced similar developments in the mid- and late-nineteenth centuries. In Japan after 1867 Emperor Meiji began a wholesale program of industrialization and urban development that encouraged wealthy landowners to consolidate holdings and hence, to remove the peasantry. In southeastern China change was initiated from without, as the European economic penetration of the densely populated valley and delta of the Pearl River placed tremendous pressures on the peasant population. In central Mexico, change came rapidly to the rural heartland of peasant agriculture after the completion of railroad lines north to the border cities in the 1890s. In contemplation of the opening of the American and Mexican urban markets to indigenous agriculture, Mexican landholders began consolidating peasant holdings, and created their own great estates of as many as forty thousand acres. Some landowners were content to sell off their increasingly valuable holdings, but while the peasantry went landless, the government of President Porfirio Diaz sought European commercial farmers to buy these lands, believing that they would achieve greater crop yields, and thus a heartier commercial agriculture, than the sustenance-oriented peasantry.

The response of the peasants to the collapse of accustomed ways of rural life was complex. They might assume traditional forms of resistance, such as riots, arson, nighttime raids, and the murder of commercial herds of sheep or cattle displacing them. Or it might take modern forms, such as rent strikes and law suits orchestrated by well-organized tenants' unions. But political protests were a difficult route, because the peasants were a declining class, acting in desperate circumstances against powerful modernizing social classes that controlled state power in all its most brutal, insidious forms.

More common were nonpolitical, individualized strategies undertaken within the framework of the family. The traditional family, with its patriarchal authority, well-defined gender roles, and insistence on the practical contributions of children effectively mobilized for common endeavor and mutual support. Younger children might be sent off to be laborers and servants. Marriage might be postponed to later ages, as in Japan and Ireland, to shorten the period of the young couple's independence and simultaneously lowering births by truncating the period of marital fertility. Family forms might be changed, too. In the European countryside, more complicated family arrangements—for example, stem families in which one son and his family might live with his parents, or joint families, in which all sons and their families lived with parents—arose for the purpose of consolidating labor, living cheaply in a common household, and meeting the challenge of paying higher rents.

Another option was migration, whether long-distance or short-distance. A high degree of transiency, especially among the young, came to characterize the peasantry. In many places, transiency had been a routine feature of the peasant economy for centuries. Younger men in particular traveled to get work, for example, helping with harvests. But, as modernizing transformations gathered force, many more people engaged in short-distance migrations, which became less about supplementing income and more about survival. Seasonal transiency might expand to encompass a larger portion of the year, as among those Scottish Highlanders who were in jeopardy of losing their leases because of the massive extension of commercial sheep farming. Some of these Scots or their sons now went to the fisheries nearly the entire year: in the winter they worked with white fish, in the spring herring in western waters, and in the summer herring in eastern waters. Nearby migrations in search of work as laborers in the new proletarianized, commercial agriculture grew common.

Exerting a more powerful pull was the vast labor market of the industrial economy in the growing cities, where technology and entrepreneurship had merged, first in textiles, to create mass production on a scale previously unimaginable. The new factory system, with its low-priced goods, simultaneously undercut the competitive position of village and town artisans and craftsmen, whose livelihoods were also imperiled by the problems that plagued their largest market, the peasantry. In consequence, traditional skilled workers joined the growing stream of migrants to cities.

It was bad enough, from his perspective, for the shoemaker to tend a machine in a shoe factory. For many peasants, a permanent descent into wage earning could only be confronted with horror. They measured value by the possession of land, whether as owners or renters, and strove to be as independent as possible in the production of the means for their survival. For peasants and traditional craftsmen to end up living the proletarian life of a wage earner in the slums of industrial cities was a miserable fate. Many millions did end up that way; without them, there would have been no European industrial revolution. Although it is difficult to know the numbers involved, rural and village folk who came to regional industrial centers might well have been engaged in step-migrations, using the wages made in factory work to finance international migration.

International migration was a strategy for avoiding proletarianization and might fill multiple practical needs: permanent resettlement; temporary work abroad while earning money to be brought back to the homeland to ensure stability in the new economy; and earning money to provide remittances sent to family at home. The extent of these remittances sent from the United States was impressive. Between 1870 and 1914, in the currency values of the day, Slovaks sent approximately $200 million home, while between 1897 and 1902 Italians sent $100 million, and between 1906 and 1930 Swedes sent $192 million. The volume of Greek remittances grew annually between 1910 and 1920 from $4.675 million to $110 million.

International migration was best considered not by the very poor, for whom it was prohibitively expensive, or by the affluent, who did not have to emigrate, but by the middle and lower-middle ranks of rural, village, and town society. They possessed the material resources to emigrate, such as fare for ships' passage and funds to aid in resettlement, but also the nonmaterial cultural capital, chief among which was literacy. This is not to say the very poor were always absent from the ranks of emigrants. Though not the poorest of their singularly immiserated society, the approximately 1.7 million Irish immigrants of the 1840s and 1850s who were victims of the potato famine were uniquely impoverished as a cohort among immigrants to the United States. Moreover, as the price of the cheapest passage declined with the coming of steamships, it became economical for poorer people to emigrate.

But understanding of the consequences of poverty must be further contextualized in the later epoch. In contrast to the situation of the resettlement of the Potato Famine Irish, who were the first generation of mass Irish Catholic emigration, by the later nineteenth century many of these poorer immigrants were members of transnational mutual support networks that bound them to family and friends already in the United States. Practical support, which might include small sums of money as well as lodging and a pre-arranged job, often compensated for lack of funds on arrival.

In the nineteenth century, when cheap, accessible land was plentiful, immigrants could dream of replicating the old way of life in the newly emerging states of the Middle West and Great Plains, where the flat prairie lands were known for remarkable fertility. Husbands and wives, with young children, in search of farmsteads were especially prominent among mid-nineteenth century Germans and Scandinavians. There were single male migrants, too, both farmers and artisans, who hoped to stay for a year or two and make enough money to return home to start families and be independent on their own land. They might work in mills, factories, or mines, even if they would not take such work in Europe. American wages were higher, and there was less reason to fear being trapped, if one had the means for returning home. Others worked in American mills in the hope of raising the capital to start farms in the United States and achieve independence of the wage economy.

Skilled workers in infant American industries were also present among the nineteenth-century immigrants, for capitalists could

10. Ole Myrvik's Sod House, Milton, North Dakota, 1896.
Scandinavian immigrants and their American-born children were
among the pioneers settling in the American Great Plains after the
Civil War. Both Ole Myrvik and his unnamed wife were children of
Norwegian immigrant parents.

not yet find among Americans the knowledge needed to operate
new industrial technologies that had emerged in Europe. In the
pioneering phase of development in a number of industries,
the importation of skilled Europeans, lured by very high wages,
was essential to achieving progress. This was the case, for
example, in brewing throughout the northern states and in
winemaking in the Ohio Valley, both of which depended on
German craftsmen, and in pottery, textiles, and stone quarrying
and cutting in which British craftsmen proved essential.

Such migrations were targeted geographically, and, if continued
over time, might lead to a virtual international integration of local
labor forces. For many years, for example, the sandstone
quarrying and cutting industry in northwestern New York State
depended partly on the importation of skilled English workers
who had been employed in the same industry in Yorkshire's
southern Pennine fringe. From the 1820s well into the twentieth
century, English cutters and quarrymen, who had been workmates

in their homelands and were introduced to their American employers by those English workers who preceded them, were migrating to work Medina sandstone in Niagara and Orleans counties. They initiated transnational employment circuits, which, in effect, simultaneously embedded them in two societies. Even in the age of sailing vessels, some migrated seasonally. They returned to Britain to divide their time between attending to small farms and quarrying and cutting at their old jobs. They might reappear to take up jobs in New York State periodically after an absence of a few years when they discovered that wages had become advantageous. Some married American women, or brought wives from England. After 1900, new immigrant Italians and Poles joined them in the quarries

The changing character of European immigration

The decline after 1890 in the reserves of arable American land that might be conveniently approached from the principal East Coast immigrant-receiving ports, the subsequent rise in the price of farm making, and the tremendous growth of mass production industries altered the character of the immigration. The demographic balance of international migration increasingly shifted from young families to single men in search in urban employment. A significant percentage of them aspired to work as long as it took in order to make enough money to return to their homelands and achieve a greater measure of independence. Men predominated two to one over women, except among the Irish. While in the international migrations of the nineteenth and early twentieth centuries women were mostly wives, mothers, and daughters arriving in family groups, the situation was different among the Irish. In Ireland women had few opportunities. Marriage was being postponed later and later, or had become impossible, as available farm land declined. But Irish women did well in American job markets, especially as domestics, because they spoke English. By the 1870s, only some 15 percent of the Irish emigration was composed of families. Irish men and women were just about equal in immigration streams to the United States between 1869 and 1920, although women outnumbered men in approximately half of those years.

The decades after 1890 were peak years for the European "birds of passage"—male transients who took advantage of transoceanic steamships to commute between their homelands and the United States. Italians were among the most transient immigrant peoples. Italian construction and agricultural laborers and railroad track maintenance workers moved routinely among the United States, Argentina, or Brazil, and their homelands. Among British workers, building artisans regularly worked both sides of the Atlantic. The principal influence of such immigrant workers was to integrate labor markets on both sides of the Atlantic.

The birds of passage must be distinguished from those noncommuting migrants who arrived with the intention of making money and leaving once and for all to fulfill aspirations in their homelands. Perhaps a quarter of those entering the United States re-emigrated. During 1908–23, approximately 89 percent of Bulgarians, Serbians, and Montenegrins, 66 percent of Romanians and Hungarians, and 60 percent of southern Italians returned to Europe. Among peoples who had little to return to because of a lack of opportunities, such as the Irish (11 percent) or because of persecution, such as the eastern European Jews (5 percent), re-emigrants were far fewer.

Nonetheless 75 percent stayed. Some men had always planned to send for their families, if they could find a promising situation. Others gradually came to the conclusion that they would be better off breaking with the past. Nonetheless, though a minority, Europeans who re-emigrated had a strong influence on the discourse of American immigration restrictionists. They sent money home rather than spend it to the benefit of American commerce. They had no desire to assimilate. The labor unions saw them as willing tools of the employers, impossible to organize.

A different picture emerged on the Pacific Coast of the United States. In these more recently settled states arable land was still available. Young Japanese immigrant families sought farmland in rural California, Washington, and Oregon. Young South Asian men from the Punjab came to the Imperial Valley of California, where large fruit and vegetable farms were being carved out of the desert in consequence of massive irrigation projects, to work as agricultural labor. Many hoped to get the money to buy small farms and form families, as some did with Mexican women, starting a unique Punjabi-Mexican hybrid ethnicity. In contrast, Mexicans displaced by consolidation of peasant landholdings by landlords first became a local agrarian proletariat, or went to work in factories and mines in northern Mexico where wages were higher than in agriculture. But spurred by the promise of even higher wages and eventually threatened by revolutionary violence, after 1900 they began entering the United States in growing numbers, across an open border, to find work in mining and agriculture in the American West.

To the casual observer mass immigration and resettlement may seem chaotic and even menacingly disorderly. But this is rarely the perception of immigrants, whose strategies for accomplishing relocation across oceans and continents have been heavily dependent on paths laid down by those often familiar individuals who came before them. Every immigration has its pioneers, whose narratives of exploration and discovery make compelling reading. But once these pioneers lay down tracks known to their families, friends, and former neighbors, even the most massive immigrant flows take on a routine, predictable character. That is the mark of the immigrant's creativity in living: in the midst of life-changing movements across vast distances, they have been guided by strategies that minimize risks and extend the realm of the familiar.

People hoping to improve themselves by pursuing work across international space have always been a highly selective group. Hard work, high aspirations, and family and group solidarity are characteristic of immigrant groups, and provide substantial resources in the struggle to make new homes.

Chapter 5

Mass population movements and resettlement, 1965 to the present

By the 1970s, when the complex pasts of the immigrant peoples of the late nineteenth and early twentieth centuries had begun to fade from memory, and they had largely achieved social and political acceptance, the United States was experiencing a third massive wave of immigration. It was made possible by the 1965 changes in immigration law, and facilitated by the loosening grip both of colonialism throughout the non-European world and of authoritarian regimes, such as the Soviet Union, the People's Republic of China, and such relatively small states as Haiti and the Dominican Republic. In 2005 the United States was the largest recipient of international migrants, taking in 1.299 million *legal* entrants. No developed nation came close to these figures: the numbers of entrants for the next five nations in rank order are Spain (569,000); Italy (225,000); Canada (208,000); Germany (200,000); and the United Kingdom (190,000). Between 2000 and 2006 alone, approximately 7.9 million immigrants, an estimated 3.7 million of whom were unauthorized, entered the United States. In those years, the total immigrant population residing in the United States equaled about 35.2 million million people, which was approximately 2.5 times larger than in 1910, the peak year of the previous mass immigration wave.

How has this massive immigration compared to the previous great migrations? While much in the world has changed since the great international migrations of the last two centuries, the underlying reasons for people to leave their homelands for far away destinations have not. Much in the nature of current of international movement is a variation on old themes enhanced by new technologies.

As in the past, contemporary migration is the consequence of the spreading out of modernizing processes, now to the developing societies of Asia, Africa, and Latin America. Population growth occasioned by decreasing mortality due to better nutrition, sanitation, and medical care, combined with the commercialization of agriculture, urbanization, and industrialization, have produced a surplus of labor in societies that cannot guarantee even educated, credentialed individuals adequate living standards and security. Political instability and war, as in Southeast Asia from the 1950s through the 1970s, Central America in the 1980s, and West Africa in the 1990s have exacerbated such socioeconomic dislocations. Rapidly evolving electronic media play the same role in disseminating knowledge of faraway alternatives that print media, personal correspondence, and the telegraph once played, and provide new cultural resources for the maintenance of immigrant networks and migration chains. Jet transportation speeds contemporary international migrants to their destinations.

While there are many international destinations for contemporary international migrants, three factors have made the United States attractive. First, there is geographic proximity, which makes immigration relatively cheap even for the poorer citizens of Mexico and the developing nations of Central and South America and the Caribbean. Second, since 1965 American immigration laws, alongside those of Canada and Australia, have been among the most welcoming in the world, even as the visa process became backlogged due to heightened security after 9/11. Third, American media and consumer goods have penetrated the world beyond Europe, globalizing visions of the American way of life. In creating rising expectations, how different is an episode of an American television program featuring alluring images of beachfront life in Miami or the dramatic lakefront skyline of Chicago from the advertisements showing endless fields of wheat on well-manicured farms that shipping lines and railroads placed in European newspapers 150 years ago? What is new is the rapidity with which knowledge spreads across the world, the astounding volume of information transmitted, and the speed and convenience with which international immigrants now reach their destinations.

While the scale of global immigration is impressive, migration remains a selective process. Most people continue to reside in the countries of their birth, and if they must relocate to seek opportunity, fulfill that need through short-distance migrations within their homelands. In 2005, when they were the leading exporters of people, Mexico and China, with emigrant populations of 797,000 and 380,000 respectively, were also in the midst of explosions of urban populations, as people in both countries left the countryside, where they could no longer survive on small farms or on farm wage labor. Mexico City, Monterrey, Shanghai, Beijing, and many other Chinese and Mexican cities have experienced explosive growth. The same migratory patterns are present in Africa, above and below the Sahara, where emigration abroad has been more than matched by massive urbanization.

The impact of contemporary immigration on the United States

While relativizing international migration in this way highlights its global nature, it may lead us to downplay its dramatic effects on contemporary America, the face of which is now being remade as dramatically as it was by the previous two mass immigration waves. There has been a nationalization of immigration, because dispersal of ethnic diversity has occurred on a scale previously unknown. Sections of the country that experienced little international migration in the past, principally the American South, are taking in large numbers of immigrants. This is a direct consequence of the shift in industrial activity after 1960 from the high-wage, unionized localities of northern and midwestern states to the low-wage, non-labor union states of the South.

The South, which historically had a vast reserve of low-wage labor in its African American population, did not experience significant European immigrant settlement, and it never had significant numbers of Hispanics. Although most Mexican migrants continue to reside in the West and Southwest, for the first time such southern states as North Carolina, Georgia, and Arkansas have significant Mexican minorities. Meanwhile, other regions, such as the Upper Midwest and the Great Plains, which had not experienced immigrant settlement since the nineteenth century, have experienced immigration again. While racial diversity was a constant throughout southern history, towns in such states as Kansas and Minnesota, experiencing the settlement of Mexicans, Somalis, Ethiopian, and Sudanese meat-packing and chicken-processing workers, had never experienced broad-scale racial diversity. Indeed for much of the history of small towns like New Ulm, Minnesota, diversity was the presence of Bohemians, Germans, Norwegians, and Swedes residing together. The ability of such peoples, white and Christian though they might be, to live side by side in spite of mutual mistrust they often brought from Europe, was once celebrated as a triumph in its own right.

The sociologist Nancy Foner has demonstrated how the two great immigration gateways, New York City and Los Angeles, serve as dramatic examples of immigration creating singular, localized patterns of diversity. New York City continues its long history of racial and ethnic diversity. As in the past, its mixture of peoples is as broad as their numbers are large. In 1920, 40 percent of its population was composed of immigrants and their American-born children; in 2000, the figure was a comparable 36 percent. New York is singular both in that it has continued to receive some of the same European immigrants, principally Poles and residents of the former Soviet Union, as in the past, and that its communities of newer, non-European immigrants in some cases build on existing populations. Its populations of foreign-born blacks originally date from a century ago when Caribbean islanders established themselves. Jamaicans, Grenadians, Haitians, and others are now joined by Africans from Senegal, Nigeria, Ghana, and elsewhere in sub-Saharan Africa. Since the 1940s, New York City has had a sizeable enough Puerto Rican population that Spanish was often heard on the streets; that population has been joined by large numbers of Hispanic peoples from throughout the Caribbean and South and Central America. The city had the largest Chinese population outside California in the twentieth century, and now the Asian population has become vastly more diverse with substantial immigrations of Korean, South Asians, and Filipinos.

California has had Mexican and Asian populations since it became part of the United States, but their legal status long placed limits on growth. In the last four decades the Los Angeles metropolitan area has been a magnet for contemporary immigration. It manifests different patterns than New York City. Like such southwestern cities as Houston, Phoenix, and Tucson, with proximity to the Mexican border, LA attracts large numbers of both legal and illegal Mexican migrants. Moreover, its relative proximity to Asia has made it attractive to transpacific migration. In addition to becoming a destination for the same Asian peoples who have settled in New York City, Los Angeles is home to America's largest concentrations of Cambodians, Laotians, and Vietnamese. A number of suburban cities and towns in the Los Angeles and San Francisco metropolitan areas have Asian majorities or near-majorities.

Significant demographic transformations are also observed in the displacement of African Americans by Hispanics as the nation's largest minority group in major American cities. Radical shifts in population ratios are taking place between African Americans and Hispanics and, with them, changes in local electoral power and cultural authority. In 1960, blacks were 20 percent and Hispanics 5 percent of the population of Houston, and in 2000, 25percent and 37 percent, respectively. In 1970, blacks were 17 percent of Los Angeles's population, but only 11 percent in 2000, while in the same three decades, Hispanics had grown from 18 percent to 47 percent. In Miami, where the Cuban population of immigrants and refugees has grown enormously since Fidel Castro's 1959 revolution, Cubans have become the largest ethnic group. Their percentage of the population grew from 24 percent to 57 percent between 1970 and 2000, while that of African Americans increased only from 15 percent to 19 percent. Where Hispanics have yet to overtake African Americans, they seem likely to do so in the near future. After New York and Los Angeles, in 2000 Chicago had the third largest Hispanic population, with 753,644 (26 percent), very largely Mexican and settled there since 1970. Hispanics were the fastest growing segment of Chicago's population. In the 1990s, with black (37 percent) and non-Hispanic white (32 percent) population growth recently falling because of suburbanization and declining birth rates, only the numbers of Hispanics rose in the midwestern city.

As the example of New York City suggests, the peoples who make up the post-1965 migration are not all strangers to America. The networks and chains that have been instrumental in forming these populations sometimes date from pre-1965 voluntary migrations. They were facilitated by national ties developed under circumstances of American colonialism; exemptions of individual countries in the Western Hemisphere from the 1924 quota legislation; and small-scale, voluntary international migration streams, such as among the Chinese. While the early Cold War facilitated the acceptance as refugees and immigrants of American allies among Taiwan Chinese, Koreans, and

Southeast Asian refugees and immigrants, it disrupted ties with Mainland China, Laos, Vietnam, and Cambodia. Not until changes in bilateral relations took place between the 1970s and 2000 did these Asian peoples immigrate to the United States in significant numbers.

The structure of contemporary immigration

International migrations continue to be constructed less along the lines of nations than social classes, genders, regions and localities, and occupations. Within these migration streams, networks and chain migrations based on family and communal relations are still the ultimate determinant of which individuals emigrate and where they resettle. The 1965 immigration law gave greater significance to the network by giving family reunification a high priority in granting visas.

How these networks and chains form and function for contemporary international migrants is seen in microcosm in the Boston area. The sociologist Peggy Leavitt has demonstrated the connections between Mira Flores, a village in the Dominican Republic, and several neighborhoods in and suburbs around Boston. Here Dominicans have been seeking work for three decades in small factories and service businesses. Using savings, some open small stores that tap the Dominican retail market. In 1994, more than 65 percent of the 545 households Mira Flores had relatives in and around Boston, and 60 percent of those households reported receiving monthly remittances from relatives in the United States. The difficulties of making a living in Mira Flores are illustrated by the fact that for 40 percent of those receiving remittances, this money was said to amount to between 75 percent and 100 percent of total household income. Similar localized connections and dependencies exist between the massive Dominican population of Washington Heights on the Upper West Side of Manhattan and people in other towns and villages in the Dominican Republic. In 1995, $796 million in remittances was sent to that Caribbean nation from the United States, and in the first eleven months of 1999, $1.4 billion. Those who re-emigrated with money earned in the United States were a substantial spur to the Dominican economy, spending their savings on consumer goods, automobiles, and homes. In 1984, 60 percent of Dominican home purchases were purchased by re-emigrants from the United States.

In social and economic terms, most contemporary international migrants come from the middle rungs of society, as in the past. Neither the rich nor the very poor, they are farmers, skilled workers, shopkeepers, teachers, accountants, office managers, building contractors, and small manufacturers. They cannot attain incomes in their homelands that allow them to buy household appliances and modern plumbing, to which they have been exposed by global mass media. Today's migration streams do depart from past immigrants, who were generally not educated beyond elementary literacy skills—and need not have been in light of the requirements (a strong back and the ability to tend a machine) of the industrializing economies of their time. Contemporary American job markets are different than in the historical past, because of the movement toward a mixed (service, technology, and manufacturing) economy. Newer immigrants are often educated and technically trained individuals, such as Asian information technology workers, with credentials to play a role in such an economy. In spite of decades of high growth and excellent public educational systems, the economies of countries such as India, Korea, and Taiwan have failed to create sufficient lucrative employment to absorb their educated younger workers, who are often forced to take low-paying jobs or consider emigration.

With its concern for domestic economic development, American immigration policy has deepened this brain drain from the developing world. The old ban on contract labor has been relaxed for skilled technical and health-related professional workers, such as nurses. If these individuals can prove that they come with prearranged jobs, the visa process is expedited. In the search for such white-collar work, English-speaking South Asians, Filipinos, and migrants from the former British Caribbean have a distinct advantage. Travel agencies and private labor recruitment agencies work hand-in-hand to facilitate the admission of these migrants. Moreover, the H-1B visa program, which created a special track for a broad array of educated technical and specialized workers, offers visas of from six to ten years duration and renewable beyond that time frame. The holder of one of these visas may seek permanent residence (through obtaining a "green card"), as many H-1B entrants have done.

As this migration stream suggests, while popular images of contemporary immigrants are of blue-collar workers, the occupational profile is more complex than ever before. A survey in 2010 found that largely because of American immigration policies and of the greater educational and skill base or the possession on arrival of some capital, the 25 million legal immigrants in the United States who live in the largest metropolitan areas—nearly two-thirds of all immigrants in the country—are almost evenly distributed across a wide continuum of occupations and incomes. In fourteen of the twenty-five largest metropolitan areas, between 51 percent and 80 percent of the immigrants are found in white-collar jobs that include business ownership and the professions. In these twenty-five large metropolitan areas, the percentage of white-collar workers among immigrants is never smaller than a third of the total of immigrants employed.

Blue-collar work continues, however, to be common among immigrants. Today's immigrants do not have access to as broad a range of stable, relatively high paying blue-collar jobs in mass production industries as in the past. Yet there is still employment for immigrants in mass production industry and in traditional factory-type settings. Jobs are sometimes found in fields in which immigrant labor traditionally worked, and where immigrants again have formed ethnic niches providing relatively reliable, if not necessarily well-paid, safe, or sanitary employment. Just as a century ago the packing houses of the great Chicago stockyards depended on thousands of eastern European Jews, Poles, Lithuanians, and Bohemians, thousands of Mexicans, Somalis, Ethiopians, and others now find work in meat-packing and chicken-processing plants. As in the past, immigrants were routed to these locations initially by recruiters, and then by people from their homelands who arrived before them.

Faced with intense international competition and subject to a relentless process of consolidation under international corporations, these plants have seen a radical compression of wages favoring low-cost immigrant labor. Wages at a representative packing plant in Oelwien, Iowa, which widely employs immigrants, fell within a few years from $18 an hour to just over $6. Another example is provided by the garment industry, which is suffering intense competitive pressure from abroad. Just as eastern European Jews and some Italians once found a niche there, whether as workers or subcontractors for larger firms, now in a much reduced American garment industry, so do Chinese immigrants in present-day New York City and Los Angeles, where they are functioning as both workers in sweatshop-like settings reminiscent of the past and as subcontractors.

Not all contemporary ethnic niches are in industry. Large numbers of Chinese and Southeast Asians own small restaurants and take-out fast food shops and perform culinary work, while Koreans operate as green grocers in New York City and Los Angeles. With personal savings or loans from relatives, Koreans sometimes come to America with the intention of opening a small store. They enhance their chances of surviving an unpredictable market by utilizing unpaid family labor, as do Chinese in the prepared food business. Grandparents are enlisted into the work force, often to watch little children, while older siblings and parents work in the family enterprise. As in the past, the ethnic market for goods and services, offered in the language of the homeland, also remains a source of opportunity for small retailers, especially in cities like Miami, Los Angeles, and New York, where immigrants groups form immense markets. But immigrants in big cities are just as engaged carving niches for themselves in small food or retailing businesses that cater to the general American market for goods and services.

This profile of the diversity of contemporary immigrant occupations suggests that even in the uncertain economy of the early twenty-first century, many immigrants have found a place for themselves or are hopeful of doing so. It is important to recall, however, that millions of immigrants are not in the country legally. While their lives are harder to track because of their status, it is clear that they do not have the same material prospects as legal residents. Illegal status limits prosperity and security; these immigrants lead a shadow existence, and risk losing not only their jobs but also property they have come to own if they are discovered and deported to their homelands.

The numerical predominance of women

That contemporary immigrant occupational streams, such as health care and sewing in garment shops, contain large numbers of adult women, especially single women, is a sharp contrast with the past. Though the extent of female numerical predominance varies greatly by group and within different areas of the country, women have made up the majority of immigrants of a number of Asian, Central and South American, and Caribbean island groups for much of the period of the recent immigration. In New York City in the early 1990s, sex ratios varied to the extent that women were a slight numerical advantage among Chinese and Dominicans, and made up as much as two-thirds of Colombian and Filipino immigrants. In sharp contrast to the past, these are wage-earning women.

A century ago, immigrant women stayed at home and their children left school to work, but today the pattern is reversed. In New York City in 1990 60 percent of immigrant women age sixteen to sixty-five were wage earning, and among the Filipinos, Jamaicans, Trinidadians, Haitians, and Guyanese—all groups profiting in the search for employment by being English-speakers—seven in ten or more were employed. Immigrant women work at all levels of employment, depending on education and technical training, from highly paid white-collar work to low-wage manufacturing and domestic and personal service, in which they have been extensively employed as nannies, nurses' helpers, and attendants in eldercare facilities.

Women's predominance in contemporary migration streams is a result of changes in American law and of the restructuring of the American economy in the last third of the twentieth century. Opportunity has become more concentrated in light manufacturing, domestic and personal service, and health care. These are traditionally women's fields, because of female traditions of caregiving and housekeeping, and gendered assumptions of employers that women are more likely to accept dead-end, low-wage, and monotonous detail work than men.

Gendered assumptions about women's work, however, do not automatically translate into low-wage work. It is true that immigrant men and women are often overqualified for the work they have to take, for technical training and higher education in one's homeland do not lead to equivalent employment, if one lacks English-language proficiency or the ability to meet American licensing and professional standards. But when training or education have been shaped to international standards in the developed world, immigrants possessing English have often succeeded in getting work commensurate with their level of preparation.

An example comes from the Philippines. Because of fear of political unrest caused by unemployment, especially among educated young people, the Philippine government after 1974 geared state and private agencies to facilitating emigration. The government was also eager to see remittance income returned to the country to spur economic development and to relieve poverty. A significant aspect of this strategy has been investment in quality nursing education to prepare women for positions abroad, so they are now to be found in relatively high-paying professional health care work in the United States. In the late twentieth century trained nurses from the English-speaking islands of the Caribbean also found extensive employment in American hospitals and eldercare facilities, especially in eastern states. In 1990, 22 percent of those (mostly women) employed in health care in New York City were from the Caribbean.

In light of the availability of such work, women have found it easier to obtain labor certifications that attest to the fact that they will be employed, and hence, to receive a visa. Consequently, in another sharp historical contrast, women have often been the pioneers in forging migration networks and chains, establishing themselves and then using family reunification programs to resettle their children and husbands. Husbands frequently lose status relative to their dominant position in the homeland. Their dependence on their wives is deepened when typically they are more often unemployed than women, or lower paid when working.

Under these circumstances, men have reluctantly become caregivers to children and housekeepers, which offends their sense of the proper order of gender relations, and results in depression, nostalgia, and desire to re-emigrate. Even though working immigrant women often continue nonetheless to perform traditional household duties, many of them are less enthusiastic about surrendering the relative independence that comes with earning their own living and American social and cultural support for gender equity. If they were to return to their homelands, they would be expected to leave the labor market and again take up full-time traditional roles. Some women, however, regard re-emigration positively, as a key to *not* having to work. They are pleased at the prospect, even if it is accompanied by the return of their husbands' traditional authority. The old role of housewife becomes acceptable, if savings from American wages enable a better living standard in a new home, with an American-style kitchen and modern appliances and plumbing.

There are many contemporary stories of women and men who were nurses, teachers, dentists, or office workers in their homelands, but for want of adequate credentials and out of economic necessity become trapped cleaning homes and offices, or doing unskilled attendant care or food service work in hospitals. They are too poor to return home and live with enhanced prosperity, but their American lives are insecure and success eludes them.

With all of the insecurity in today's American job markets, which exacerbates the risk-taking inherent in immigration, it is logical to ask what immigrants gain, especially those who commit themselves to staying permanently in the United States. A century ago many newcomers could at least count on some evidence of rapid improvement, if only relative to the miserable circumstances they had left behind. In confronting the paradox of choosing downward mobility, it is necessary to remember the strategizing, pragmatic mentality characterizing modern international migrants.

In spite of its attendant difficulties, immigration is judged a better long-term solution to the problem of achieving an acceptable, secure standard of living than remaining at home. While the immigrant generation might experience disappointment, parents may convince themselves that their children will eventually live better than they do. They sustain these hopes even as they worry about the exposure of young people in America to drugs, gangs, violence, sexual license, and antisocial attitudes challenging the authority of clergy, parents, teachers, and police. As in the past, immigration remains a gamble, and resettlement a tentative process that demands the energy and intelligence of those who choose to give up their old homes to improve themselves in new ones.

Part III

The dialogue of ethnicity and assimilation

Throughout American history, there has been anxiety over a perceived unwillingness of immigrants to become Americans. The public expressions of this anxiety seem very similar from one era to another, even as the origins of the immigrants and the circumstances of their migrations have changed. A widely discussed statement of this position that has been influential among both the lay public and policymakers is the political scientist Samuel P. Huntington's *Who Are We?: The Challenges to America's National Identity* (2004). The author contends that contemporary immigrants, especially the large number of working-class Mexicans, are poor candidates for American citizenship and do not wish to assimilate. Huntington's work may be rhetorically free of the gross, explicit prejudices that have been prompted in some anxious popular analysts by the declining numerical superiority of whites, as Asian and Hispanic immigrant populations grow and complement the African American minority. It nonetheless reads much like the polemics written in the mid-nineteenth century that made the same points about those ultimately most assimilated of ethnics, the Irish. Later, heavily influenced by race thinking, the same charges once made against the Irish were leveled at the Chinese, Japanese, Jews, Italians, Slavs, Greeks, and others.

Past or present, there have been at least two related problems with such arguments. They have depended, first, on the assumption that the immigrant's *ethnicity* is evidence of a willful, abiding separateness, and not of a desire for a supportive communal affiliation and sustaining identity amid the psychological, cultural, and social challenges of emigration and resettlement. Second, they proceed on the dubious, essentialist assumption that there is an unchanging core American culture and identity, descended directly out of colonial British stock and the Founding Fathers of American nationhood, which one must embrace to be a real American. While the founders created an excellent model for the government of a democratic republic and abiding institutions that have made that model durable, this hardly implies that all Americans can or should possess a character menu composed of the same traits. In reality, if there is a core American-ness, over the centuries it has come to reside in a live-and-let-live commitment to a combination of diversity and support for the constantly debated American creed composed of practical principles for getting along in daily life amid the pursuit of opportunity. One of the tenets of that creed has been the freedom to maintain a distinctive identity, even while adopting the common behaviors and attitudes needed to attain prosperity and security.

When immigrants have reflected on the charge that they are not real Americans, it must be a source of considerable confusion. All around them has been diversity of peoples, manners, mores, origins, memories, or experiences. Who are the real Americans, and where does one find them? How long does it take to be admitted to their ranks? What qualifies one for admission? As these nebulous questions indicate, it is ultimately a frustrating discussion that easily lapses into exasperation or bigotry. It is legitimate to debate how many immigrants should be admitted to the United States, or whether at any given time it is in the national interest to admit any. It is quite another matter to sort out people by ascribed characteristics that predict whether they will possess or lack an essence that is somehow American. Yet such a tendency has been present throughout the American experience of immigration, especially when significant cultural and racial differences are perceived.

These assumptions about both ethnicity and authentic American-ness have produced a fear-ridden mentality that underestimates the capacities of American society to form a nation out of so many distinctive groups. Immigrants pursue opportunity, the raison d'être for voluntary migratory behavior, and in their minds America has long been a place for realizing that possibility. The dynamic engine that has been the American economy—combined with the constitutional framework of rights protecting the individual in the attributes of citizenship and the possession of property—has been both a magnet for immigrants and a guarantor of their willingness to adopt common American behaviors and attitudes. In pursing their aspirations, immigrants have utilized the tools at hand, whether within themselves, their families, and their ethnic groups, or American society, to acquire education, skills, and credentials, pursue better paying employment, improve their standard of living, and enhance individual and family security. They adopt behaviors and attitudes that advance their goals, such as learning English, the language of American opportunity. In doing so they not only improve themselves, but they also simultaneously assimilate into American society, as they understand it. For them, America is a place where dreams may be realized, if you follow the broad paths laid down before you.

Assimilation has been aided not only by American prosperity and by laws that evolved over time toward inclusiveness and fairness, but also by a gradually widening mainstream that has been accommodated these aspirations. The mainstream is that societal location where individuals find access to all the resources—most critically, work, a place of residence, education, and rights under law—that guarantee a decent standard of living and material security. Access to the mainstream is protected by laws and institutional rules that have come increasingly to guarantee equality in the competition for resources. To seek inclusion in that mainstream is to put oneself in a position to assimilate, whether or not that is a conscious goal. "Assimilation is something that frequently enough happens to people," say the sociologists Richard Alba and Victor Nee, "while they are making other plans."

Assimilation is not a one-way street for the newcomer but, over time, a process of mutual accommodation among all elements of society. Features of individual ethnic groups are not easily found in American society. It is not possible to say with confidence, for example, what is Italian or Chinese or Mexican or Jewish about America. Instead it is diversity itself, in the sense of accommodating cultural and identificational differences, which is embedded in America. To be sure, the most obvious, visible accommodations are those of the immigrants, but society itself has continually been changed by the presence of such diversity. All individuals and the groups to which they belong may bring to this mainstream distinctive identities, memories, and histories that inform behavior and understanding, so that in the process of cultural and social homogenization as people pursue opportunity, Americans remain heterogeneous in their conception of who they are. A national statement of faith, *E Pluribus Unum* (Out of Many, One) appears, appropriately enough, on America's money, the symbol of American opportunity. The motto is true enough, but paradoxically only as long as the observer does not expect the many to disappear as they become one, or the one to look exactly the same from one historical era to another. Ethnicity and assimilation remain in dialogue continually throughout the American experience of diversity.

Chapter 6
The widening mainstream

In the early twentieth century Henry Ford sponsored citizenship and language classes at his Michigan automobile factories, which depended heavily on immigrant labor. The climactic moment in the graduation ceremony was when individual immigrants, with placards around their necks or small flags in their hands that identified their homelands, mounted the stage and walked into a giant wooden kettle labeled "melting pot." After emerging on the other side of the kettle, the placard or flag was gone, and each held a small American flag in his hand. They were now Americans.

Around the same time, the University of Chicago sociologists William I. Thomas and Florian Znaniecki, who were pioneers along with their Chicago colleagues in the academic study of immigrants, offered an influential explanation for why such a ceremony was based on simplistic wishful thinking. They found that immigrants developed their own group life and identities, and that all efforts, well-meaning or malign, to speed them rapidly into an assimilation that effaced their pasts were doomed to fail because they were conceived outside the immigrants' own experiences and needs. They wrote in the midst of a political climate in which large numbers of native-stock Americans demanded immigrant political and cultural conformity in the name of "Americanization." Americanization might mean the

11. The graduation ceremony at the Ford automobile factory English School in which the graduates entered a simulated melting pot, often holding flags or having placards around their necks that identified their native lands, and emerged holding American flags.

suppression of foreign language newspapers, as many local and state governments demanded during World War I, or it might mean the generally benign efforts of employers, school teachers, and social workers to teach what they deemed American citizenship, manners, and beliefs alongside the English language. Whatever the form of such cultural instruction, the two sociologists believed it would probably, at best, have only a superficial influence on immigrant identities. At worst, if insensitively enforced and accompanied by derision for the immigrants' cultures, it might create hostility to assimilation and animosity toward Americanizers.

Documented in what became a classic study of Polish immigration as well as a template for understanding the problems all modern voluntary immigrants faced in resettlement, their assumptions were based on understandings of how human beings confront all-encompassing transformations that shake the very foundations of their world. In the midst of the social disorganization and individual demoralization that came with leaving the land, emigrating, and resettling in the industrial cities of the United States, these immigrants created "a new society," neither completely Polish nor completely American. Its purpose was mutual support, consolation, and continuity in the midst of the struggles to fulfill material aspirations. In other words, like the immigrants of the past and those entering the country alongside the Poles, they formed an *ethnic group*, with its own institutions, such as churches and mutual aid societies, informal social networks based upon family, neighborhood, and community, and an identity based on common experience, memory, language, and history.

In light of its elementary, sustaining functions, ethnicity has been a phenomenon common to all immigrant groups. While the most racialized voluntary immigrant groups, such as the Chinese, Japanese, and Mexicans, had their cultures disrupted by prejudice, legal and social discrimination, and violence, within the enclave communities they created their ethnic groups had many of the same functions one might observe among peoples who were more widely accepted. Efforts to interfere with the group and individual processes of ethnicity are more or less futile. People cannot live successfully, in comfort with themselves or with others, without some continuity of self-understanding, personal relations, and sources of self-worth. Would the result then be an America where people could not know one another, and in which revered institutions of government and society were destined to die? Would Americans become strangers in their own land? Not according to Thomas and Znaniecki and other University of Chicago sociologists, for they were the original sources of the crucial understanding of assimilation as not simply a process of the immigrants becoming Americans, but ultimately of mutual accommodation, in which society changes alongside the changing individuals and groups that compose it.

Immigrant accommodation has taken place at the individual, group, and institutional levels. Little that immigrants do after leaving their homelands can realistically be construed as foreign. Especially in the necessary daily acts of working, creating a household, and functioning in the marketplace, immigrants must learn new rules and new behaviors. Immigrant generation parents often struggle mightily to master these new ways; their self-transformation is rendered more difficult because it must be accomplished in adulthood. In contrast, their American-raised children learn them more easily, though not without occasional pain, both at school, which has been the central site for formal socialization in modern society, and informally, on the streets among peers. School teaches the official version of American society, and the streets, the rules for coexisting and gaining advantage in ordinary interactions.

Ethnicity may mask this process of accommodation by highlighting difference, but ethnicity has not only been about preserving an old identity. It also has been a central agent of assimilation, because the ethnic group is among the principal sites for absorbing the new rules and behaviors necessary for the immigrants to fulfill their aspirations. Within the ethnic group, learning American ways by taking instruction from fellow ethnics has occurred with less pressure, ridicule, and rejection, and hence fewer penalties and less humiliation for being an inadequate student. Immigrants also have learned lessons from longer-resident ethnic groups. In this role the Irish have loomed especially large in oral tradition, because they were relatively slow to prosper, and lived longer in the proletarian neighborhoods that received recently arrived groups. Their length of American residence made the Irish veterans in the processes of ethnicity and assimilation, and assisted them, along with their knowledge of English, in obtaining political power at the neighborhood and municipal levels. In the eyes of newcomers, they possessed authority about getting along in America. Ironically, the Irish embodied America for many newcomers.

The lessons learned have not been the official formulation of American values and ways. They contain much practical realism about class inequalities of power and wealth, and the ordinary corruption of government. They constitute recognition that for all the bright promises America offers, one must never trust that it is everything patriots say about it.

Individuals seeking opportunity

Ethnic fiction develops narratives that vividly portray these painful transitions. In such stories of immigrant experience as Mario Puzo's *The Fortunate Pilgrim* (1964), Pietro DiDonato's *Christ in Concrete* (1939), Abraham Cahan's *The Rise of David Levinsky* (1917), Anzia Yezierska's *Breadgivers* (1925), and Amy Tan's *The Joy Luck Club* (1989), the same themes reappear, from male and female perspectives and across group lines. Informed by the authors' personal experiences as young immigrants or as the American-born children of immigrants, these narratives relate to a common theme: the aspirations for a liberated self, given hope by American opportunities, but frustrated by the constraints of poverty and Old World traditions rendered dysfunctional in a new land. Associated with the difficulties in realizing this aspiration is often a conflict between parents who defend tradition and children who seek to embrace the future.

The fictional characters move painfully toward finding a place for themselves within America. It is not necessarily the place they had aspired to, as in the case of DiDonato's Paul, a sensitive young man with intellectual yearnings for truths beyond the consolations of his mother's peasant Catholic piety. He must work a construction job after his father's death in a work accident. He sees his hopes for attaining an education snatched from him by the family burdens he must assume. Or, they find that what they thought they aspired to turns out to be hollow, as in case of Cahan's David Levinsky, who wants to be rich, uses American opportunities to become so, and is disappointed that it does not make him happy. Or, as in the case of Yezierska's Sarah and Tan's Chinese daughters, they may transform themselves into independent American women, only to find that a complete break with the past is neither possible nor desirable. But to the extent these fictional characters consider it their right to transform themselves, they represent the energies born of American opportunities.

Often lacking as a major plot element are struggles by the major characters against prejudice and discrimination. This is hardly because prejudice and discrimination have been absent. For the immigrants, social acceptance and a full range of opportunities came more grudgingly than the chance to make a living at a low-wage job and to set down roots. But strategies for dealing with whatever forces limited opportunity, without having to challenge them directly from a position of relative weakness, seem always to have been available to individuals, and were often successful in providing at least partial relief. If barred from skilled building trades by antisemitic discrimination, as they were in a number of cities, Jews had other avenues of opportunity in small business, owning corner grocery stores and discount clothing stores. They had an ethnic niche in the garment industry, in which Jews owned firms that used Jewish subcontractors and hired co-ethnics. All apparel-making businesses, independent of the owner's ethnic identity, looked for experienced, skilled pressers, sewing machine operators, and fancy stitch makers, who were widely found among the immigrant Jews.

Enclave economies also provided opportunity for the Chinese, who faced significant employment discrimination. They, too, developed their own niche in the apparel industry. They also profited from the exoticization of American Chinatowns, in which they opened restaurants, bars, nightclubs, and brothels for non-Chinese consumers, and employed their own people to work in them. In contrast to such urban employment niches, the Japanese in western states created a space for themselves in vegetable and fruit farming and landscaping, in which they founded successful family enterprises, using family labor and that of wage labor from their own ethnic group. Barred from owning land by discriminatory legislation, these immigrants often arranged to have their property placed in the legal control of their American-born children. Their ownership might survive internment during World War II, though local officials sometimes destroyed records proving ownership, and neighbors entrusted with guardianship took advantage of the situation to seize property.

A key question for understanding assimilation is whether such ethnic niches might become a permanent trap. This did not happen. Later generations have not wished to enter these occupations, which seemed parochial, limiting, and embodiments of ethnic stereotypes they wished to shed in order to become more American. While they might provide security, they paid relatively poorly and offered fewer chances for advancement. In the twentieth century, strategies were devised, often employing education, to enter public employment, the professions, or corporate business. When they encountered discrimination in admissions to private higher educational institutions, they turned to public colleges, universities, and graduate schools. The number of these public institutions grew greatly after 1945 to accommodate millions of World War II veterans, who took advantage of generous government programs to obtain higher education, and later the postwar baby boom generation. While discrimination might be encountered in private sector job markets, government served as a substitute, especially as the role in society of the state, at all levels, expanded in the immediate postwar decades. Federal government programs subsidized the acquisition of single-family housing and made it affordable for many to leave crowded older neighborhoods for the emerging urban fringe areas.

The barriers presented by discrimination also appeared increasingly permeable in the private sector. The American economy expanded so dramatically after 1945 that significant shortages of skilled, educated, and credentialed workers were present everywhere. With enough opportunity available for everyone, the old prejudices were gradually relaxed, and alongside them the old barriers to mutual accommodation. Indeed for millions of European ethnics the types of discrimination they often encountered in the immediate postwar decades, in private businessmen's clubs, golf clubs, and resort hotels and in suburban housing markets, were artifacts of their growing prosperity. They were efforts to impede upwardly mobile people from making their presence felt in places where they had been absent. Those barriers, too, eventually greatly declined, and where social acceptance lagged, individuals often chose not to care, protected by ethnicity and by the force of their own ambitions. They might also adopt such *passing* strategies as name changes and false family histories.

Yet the American mainstream itself widened greatly in the second half of the twentieth century. Common enrollment in public colleges and universities, and common residence in the suburbs created new, shared patterns of life among diverse peoples. Of key importance, too, was a dramatic national self-examination spurred by various civil rights movements based on race and various liberation movements based on gender, sexual orientation, and disability. As it did, the circle of "We" in conceiving of the identity of Americans widened significantly. Passing soon became an embarrassing remnant of self-hatred. By the 1970s ethnic origins were being widely celebrated and publicly asserted. Immigrant peoples who had been read out of history were now being credited with significant contributions, such as the critical role Chinese railroad laborers played in building the transcontinental railroad. Historic wrongs were admitted and official apologies rendered. In 1988 Congress passed and President Ronald Reagan signed legislation apologizing for Japanese internment and appropriating more than $1.6 billion in reparations for those interned or their heirs. Some argued that such actions were too little—done too late, but it is very difficult to argue that national denial of embarrassing facts and terrible wrongs is a better course to follow.

Institutions come to embody diversity: labor unions and electoral politics

The widening mainstream was also the result of processes through which ethnic groups *as groups,* and hence diversity itself, came to be integrated into American society. Without an ancient feudal inheritance to guide its passage into modernity, the United States was invented from the ground up, especially when it came to the relationship between its diverse peoples. This is evident in electoral politics and the labor movement, both of which highlight the ways in which basic American social processes and institutions were shaped in the nineteenth and twentieth centuries around the necessity of accommodating difference.

The American labor movement has been a tentative achievement. It was slow historically to organize and win recognition. It is vulnerable in the current age of globalization, because of the erosion of employment among its members, as overseas and domestic nonunion competition undercut the mighty mass production industries of the mid-twentieth century. Organized labor reached the height of its power around 1945, when the federal government encouraged unionization for the sake of efficient war production, and approximately 36 percent (14.5 million) American workers were unionized. While smaller than the percentage of organized workers in other advanced capitalist democracies at the time, organized labor nonetheless had substantial influence and power in politics and the industrial economy, especially in such key sectors as garments, consumer electronics, household appliances, automobiles, steel, rubber, and chemicals. It was a dependable part of the Democratic coalition that controlled national politics between the 1930s and the 1970s, and successfully advanced a social democratic program for government in society. With job losses in basic industries after 1980, as the fortunes of organized labor declined—about 14.7 million workers (11.9 percent) were unionized late in 2010—so, too, did the Democratic Party. The numbers belie organized labor's contemporary importance, for it is especially prominent in the dynamic public employment sector.

The tentativeness of labor unionism's achievements has many causes, but one that looms especially large historically, alongside the great diversity of the economy and the size of the country, is the cultural diversity of the workforce, especially its immigrant character. The immigrants understood the virtues of solidarity. Ethnic group formation was premised on collective action in such endeavors as forming burial societies, churches, and sectarian school systems (for Catholics, Lutherans, and Orthodox Jews) as alternatives to state-funded schools. Large numbers of immigrant workers, especially the nineteenth-century English, Scots, and Germans, had already experienced the class conflict, radical politics, and union organizational campaigns born of protests against proletarianization during the industrial revolution in Europe. But while many experiences taught the value of solidarity, immigration itself was ultimately based on individual initiative and individual and family aspirations. During the most sustained drive to form mass production industries, immigrant workers were enabled by the revolution in transoceanic transportation to make money and quickly return home. Organizing campaigns and prolonged strikes were an impediment to these aspirations. When provoked by employer actions such as reneging on wage agreements, even these birds of passage might react with a job action, but these short, sudden spasms of militancy did not create a labor movement.

Thus, though voluntary immigration was entirely about material rewards, it did not necessarily inspire worker solidarity in pursuit of those rewards. Observing immigrant behavior, unions saw most immigrants as unorganizable and an impediment to labor's progress. Furthermore, most unions in the late nineteenth and early twentieth centuries represented skilled craft workers. In contrast, the immigrants were for the most part unskilled workers, merely machine tenders on assembly lines or outdoor construction laborers. If they worked in the same industries with skilled unionized workers, they were not represented by their unions and did not share their wage scales. Unions of skilled workers also were, by and large, made up of native-stock white workers and the northern and western European ethnics who were long settled in America. A good deal of nativist contempt for foreigners frequently informed their response to recent eastern, central, and southern European immigrants, people of dubious whiteness, who seemed willing to take any sort of abuse to make a dollar. Asians, Mexicans, blacks, and other non-whites inspired even greater hostility. The occasional use of immigrant workers as strikebreakers hardened the view that immigrants were poor union material.

What was needed was a new union movement, which simultaneously reached out to all workers and organized workers by industry, not by skill level, in the interests of both collective power and countering the use of immigrants to break strikes and wage scales. Skilled workers, too, knew that they could be replaced by a new machine worked by an unskilled immigrant, especially if the latter felt no sense of moral obligation to them and was not bound by union discipline.

The impediments to the development of this sort of unionism were many, not the least of them the distrust among ethnic groups and the power of employers when supported, as they frequently were, by state power in the form of both court injunctions against striking unions and use of state militias and federal troops to protect strikebreakers and break picket lines. Yet gradually during the first half of the twentieth century in one mass production industry after another, unions with strong multi-ethnic, and ultimately multiracial, foundations were formed. These unions did not deny cultural differences but respected them, and balanced them off against a common commitment to American values of fairness and equality and to class solidarity. While immigrant and ethnic workers, such as Mexican and Filipino agricultural laborers and Chinese, Jewish, and Italian garment workers, showed considerable initiative in organization campaigns when encouraged to participate, leadership in union organizing often came from the more class-conscious elements of American and older ethnic group workers, who were the veterans of past struggles. Walter and Victor Reuther, the sons of German immigrant socialists, spent their lives in the labor movement and were instrumental in the formation of the multi-ethnic, multiracial United Auto Workers. A similar evolution toward inclusiveness may be traced in the United Steelworkers of America, whose founder and first president, Philip Murray, was born in Scotland, and in the United Rubber Workers, whose first president, Sherman Dalrymple, a native-born Anglo-American, was raised on a farm in West Virginia. Recognition in apportioning union offices and leadership positions in the workplace on negotiation committees or as shop stewards was proof of the willingness of such union leaders to reach out to immigrant workers. Thus, a vital element of American social democracy emerged out of multicultural foundations. It continues to do so. After internal debates that closely resembled those of the past, sectors of the American labor movement have once again become committed to organizing immigrant workers, such as the large numbers of women employed in housekeeping by corporate hotel chains.

A similar societal evolution took place in electoral politics, though much more rapidly. The stakes in American elections, especially at local levels, have always been greater than the offices contested, because the victor has taken control of public resources, especially government jobs, which might be apportioned to friends, family, and electoral supporters. Proudly self-conscious heirs of the Founding Fathers, native white Americans rarely saw it that way, believing elections were not about opportunity but about principles and ideas. Early in the history of American elections, however, as the electorate swelled beyond the narrow ranks of substantial property holders through democratization of the franchise by the individual states, politicians came to understand that political patronage in the form of jobs was a useful tool in mobilizing plebian supporters.

They also came to understand that it was impossible to mobilize a mass electorate one voter at a time. What was needed was a way of approaching the voters as members of groups with their own leaders, who might become simultaneously clients of politicians and power brokers in their own right. From the arrival of the Irish, Germans, and various groups of Scandinavians in the mid-nineteenth century, political parties came to see the advantage of mobilizing ethnic leadership and voters to form electoral majorities. The numbers of immigrants seemed endless, and after only five years of American residence, they were entitled to become citizens and hence to vote. For their part, ethnics proved disciplined voters, if offered incentives. Solidarity in electoral politics came easier to the immigrants and their descendents than it did to Anglo-Americans, whose belief in principled individualism made them slower to recognize group interests. Ethnic groups voted undeviatingly for the party of their choice, often for many decades. Scandinavians were longtime proud Republicans. Irish Americans were Democratic loyalists and party leaders at every level for well over a century. Jews have been among the most solidly Democratic of the white ethnic groups for decades. Superimposed on these ethnic preferences has been a succession process, by which each new wave of immigration has displaced the previous one in positions of party leadership.

In return for votes, politicians promised a variety of symbolic recognitions and benefits, and the ethnic groups discovered a new, fortuitous path to fulfilling their aspirations. In addition to nominations to office and public employment, there has been assistance to communities in the form of such social services as neighborhood public schools, police protection, public health programs, and parks and recreational facilities. Also, there was support on issues such as the long-abiding conflict over the social control of alcohol, in which many immigrants, possessing European standards of tolerance for drinking and ethnic cultures that revolved around the social uses of alcohol, were aligned against American Evangelical Protestants, who saw the use of alcohol as sinful and a source of social disorder.

The gradual progress of civil service reform led to apportioning most public employment through objective measures of fitness determined by job experience and performance on standardized tests, and undercut patronage politics. Yet ethnic bases for mobilizing the American electorate abide, because politics still apportions a variety of resources and recognitions along partisan lines.

Another long-standing function of ethnic politics has concerned homeland affairs, and because it is transnational in its reach, it has always been especially controversial. As a source of controversy, however, it, too, suggests the mutual accommodations by which American pluralism has been formed. Among these homeland issues have been not only demands for changes in immigration restrictions and support for increased numbers of refugees, but also in matters directly involving American foreign policy, such as support for opposition to international aggression or for homeland liberation. There is a long list of instances in which pressure has been exerted through the power of ethnic votes. These efforts emerged first with the nineteenth-century Irish. Soon after attaining significant numbers in politics in the 1850s, they organized a strong effort on behalf of American support for liberation of Ireland from British rule. An Irish campaign about homeland affairs continued through the creation of the Irish Free State in 1921 and the independent Republic of Ireland in 1949, and would ultimately include the question of control of Northern Ireland and support for the Catholic rights protests there in the late twentieth century.

The Irish have not been alone in using their vote and the possession of free speech as a wedge to influence American law and policy. Poles and Slovaks wanted support for independent homelands before and during World War I. During the Cold War, a wide variety of Eastern and Central European ethnics pressured the American government to free their homelands from Soviet control. Jews hoped to influence American refugee policy in the 1930s, so that more visas were issued to those wishing to flee Germany and, after the creation of Israel in 1948, began a decades-long effort on behalf of government support for Israel's security. To combat that effort, Arab Americans, whose numbers have grown since 1965, mobilized their votes behind politicians sympathetic to the Palestinians. Italian Americans in the two decades after World War II organized to obtain increases in the admission of Italian immigrants and refugees above quota levels. Since the Cuban Revolution of 1959, Cuban Americans have used their large numbers in South Florida to influence American refugee policy and to support the American economic boycott of Cuba.

Such transnational ethnic political actions have been criticized on the grounds that the groups involved manifest disloyalty—or sometimes, more generously stated, unresolved dual loyalties. Yet ethnic activism of this type actually has drawn ethnic groups into the American mainstream, while widening that mainstream to legitimize their presence and concerns. The Irish, for example, became more American in substantial measure through decades of advocacy for their homeland, and the same dynamic process can be seen in other American ethnic groups, from Europeans in the past to contemporary Tibetans and Rwandans. When criticized by Americans for conflicted loyalties, Irish Americans justified their activism saying they were demonstrating their *American* patriotism. They explained that the ideal situation for a liberated Ireland would be for it to adopt the values and institutional models of the American polity. Involvement in the processes of politics, moreover, integrated the Irish into the political party system and taught them to present their issues to those outside their group and to lobby the American government. It was no contradiction in the minds of Irish Americans that their St. Patrick's Day parades routinely gave representation simultaneously to symbols of American loyalty and Irish nationalism.

Across the continent, the same phenomenon manifested itself in the San Francisco area in the 1930s and 1940s, as Chinese Americans assumed a public role as advocates for China in its struggle against Japanese aggression. Voting was of less consequence than among the Irish, because there were far fewer Chinese citizens, and they were concentrated in a small number of electoral districts. But through large, well-planned public rallies, parades, and demonstrations, they influenced American policy and public opinion. Chinese American women worked through their labor union, the Independent Ladies Garment Workers Union, to organize a boycott of Japanese goods. During the war, they joined the American women's armed forces in significant numbers in order to play a role in defeating Japan.

Such examples of cohesive pluralism demonstrate the power of ethnicity simultaneously to strengthen the group and to assist it in speeding its way into the mainstream. America has not always enthusiastically welcomed immigrants. But its homogenizing social and political arrangements have created opportunities for them to become a part of an American society that becomes more unified and hence stronger because of the integration of diverse peoples, who retain their differences, even as they come to act and think in common.

Chapter 7
The future of assimilation

Pessimistic projections

Because American institutions have been shaped around accommodating difference, the absorptive capacities of American society have been formidable. Yet some articulate contemporary observers believe those powers have ended and that the current mass immigration is speeding their demise. The most articulate and well known of these observers among conservatives is Samuel P. Huntington. If present immigration trends continue, America will lose what Huntington believes to be its "core Anglo-Protestant culture." This culture, he argues, has made it uniquely successful among nations in world history and has been the source of social order. Bereft of its unifying identity, America will then suffer cultural balkanization and perhaps eventually physical fragmentation. Huntington's influence in shaping popular discourse and debate on immigration lies in the fact that in dramatic projections of this type he effectively articulates anxieties that lie just below the surface of a large sector of American opinion.

Huntington echoes the nativism of a century ago, but he is quick to attempt to separate himself from the racialized bigotry that often characterized it. America does not need "Anglo-Protestants" to survive, he maintains; it needs the public culture they created.

Creed, not genes will determine its future. Immigrants in the past, he argues, remade themselves in the image of Anglo-Protestantism, while those today refuse to, and in a political climate enamored by the vision of a postnational, globalized world order, they are not required to do so. For Huntington, the greatest threat to the continuity of America as a self-governing democratic society lies in recent immigrants who seem to him to be unenthusiastic about assuming the responsibilities of American citizenship.

This pessimistic vision rests on faulty but not uncommon assumptions. For Huntington, American public culture, *Anglo-Protestantism* as reflected in the nation's laws, system of governance, and social values, seems frozen in time, unchanging in its essence since the dawn of the United States. With its hunger for an idealized, much simplified past, such an argument defies the logic of modern history. In the modern world, with its incessant pace of change, historical processes never stop evolving, and no place, however once remote, has been free of being swept along by such transformations. A half-century after the American Revolution, the United States had already begun its transformation from the underpopulated, provincial society of farmers, artisans, and slave-owning planters of the Founding Fathers to an urban, industrial world power. As early as the 1840s, that transformation began to be reflected in the frequent remaking of the American workforce and American institutions, such as political parties, by immigration. Multicultural diversity has not simply been the by-product of change; it is constitutive of the very processes of change and hence of American society itself.

To be sure, for Huntington the contemporary failure of assimilation is based on a substantive historical transition in the character of immigrants. Immigrants, he assumes, are no longer required to and increasingly do not care to assimilate. Faced with the choice, they decline. Unlike past immigrants, they do not want to be a part of America. They go back and forth across borders, especially the porous Mexican border, with little concern for the problems or future of American society. The formal exercise of citizenship is irrelevant to them.

There are indeed those present-day immigrants who, like the birds of passage of the past, have no intention of resettling permanently, and may be charged, just as those migrants were a century ago, with using the United States as a cash machine. Yet this familiar charge overlooks, as it did in the past, the value of the work they do while they are in the United States, which is from the practical standpoint of most lawmakers why they are encouraged to immigrate. The international search for opportunity is easier than it was a century ago, because of the ongoing pace of economic globalization and technological change in transportation and communication. Moreover, as in the past but on an even broader scale, governments, including that of the United States, encourage transnationality by recognizing dual citizenship, and easing the transfer of money, property, and capital between homelands and lands of resettlement.

In the scale and ease of such itinerancy, the world may indeed be a different place than it was during the previous population movements that critics of contemporary immigration find did not challenge the Anglo-Protestant culture they revere—although one could never have convinced the nativists of the past that those immigrations were not crises in their own right. Nation-states will probably never again reside in isolation from the moment-to-moment workings of world labor and capital markets. There is equally little doubt that itinerant workers, managers, and entrepreneurs, with cosmopolitan attitudes that leave them more or less indifferent to the history and memory of the places in which they reside for employment, will be present in unprecedented numbers everywhere there is opportunity, whether in Dubai, France, Venezuela, or the United States.

On the other hand, recent American immigration law has encouraged the reconstruction of families, which make up a substantial portion of contemporary immigration. The children of these immigrant families grow up in a new society, attend its schools, and form their peer groups in their neighborhoods and schools. America is the only world they know. Throughout the history of American immigration, a common impediment to the re-emigration of immigrant parents has been the disposition of their children to continue to live the only life they know, an American one. When immigrant parents take these children to the ancestral homeland for a visit in order to acquaint them with its culture, language, and landscape, the principal result is that the children come to a conscious understanding of just how American they are.

Thus, fundamental elements of their situation, such as a well-paying job, home ownership, or parenthood of Americanizing children, work to direct even those immigrants inclined to return to their homelands toward assimilation. Assimilation has never been simply a matter of the formal oaths of the naturalization process or about assuming or declining an identity. Immigrants and their children must involve themselves in socioeconomic processes that move them and their families toward the mainstream, for it is in their interest to learn American behaviors and attitudes in pursuing their own aspirations. There is no cultural essence to be internalized; there is instead a life to be lived and material aspirations to be realized.

Significant questions have been raised about whether the daily social and economic processes of assimilation that direct immigrants and their children into the mainstream are themselves working as effectively as in the past. One set of concerns legitimately arises out of the volume of illegal immigration. Unauthorized immigrants encounter the threat of legal prosecution that imperils their ability to reside and work in the United States, inhibits property ownership and family security, and retards their ability to attain wage equality with legal residents. While there has always been illegal immigration, numbers in the early twenty-first century, perhaps as many as 12 million during 2000–2010, dwarf anything thought to have previously existed. Many employers have come to depend on this source of cheap labor, and employ it to free themselves from the burden of negotiating with unions and paying the costs of such worker benefits as health insurance. Moreover, unauthorized immigrants, as consumers and taxpayers, have become significant elements of local and regional economies. Even in a state like Ohio, far from the nation's southern border and not a major destination for immigrants (about 3.7 percent of population in 2007), has a significant investment in unauthorized workers. A study in that year by the Immigration Policy Center estimated that the state's economy would lose up to $4 billion in consumer spending, $1.8 billion in economic output, and approximately 25,000 workers, if unauthorized immigrants were removed. In Colorado, with an immigrant population totaling 10 percent, unauthorized immigrants are estimated by the same organization to have paid between $159 million and $194 million in state and local taxes in 2005, some of which has helped fund those programs, such as unemployment insurance, that they are barred by law from using.

This morally and politically untenable situation breeds exploitation and profound inequalities, strains law enforcement, and fosters contempt for law. Options for resolving it include guest-worker programs, tougher and consistently enforced employer penalties for hiring illegal immigrants, enhanced border security, and an expedited path to citizenship for those unauthorized immigrants who desire it. Political paralysis has blocked action. The issue involves border security in an age of international terrorism, the bilateral relations between Mexico and the United States, the prosperity of important industries, the livelihoods of American workers, and tolerance of lawbreaking. Thus, it simultaneously carries great practical, symbolic, and emotional weight, with political risks for those who seek to resolve it.

If illegal immigration were successfully addressed, it would still be necessary to address another set of concerns: Are the relevant social and economic processes leading immigrants into the mainstream working successfully for the majority—the legal contemporary immigrants—whose ranks the former illegals might then join? We might also ask whether these same processes worked evenly and invariably in the past. If the contemporary situation is indeed unprecedented and beyond American experience, it may well be seen as a cause for despair.

For conservatives, the key to their prediction that immigrants will not assimilate lies in cultural differences that will inevitably breed disorder. Analysts on the Left, who are more sympathetic to the immigrants, are interested in equality and social justice more than in social order. But they, too, see a threat to assimilation. What is crucial for their analysis is the question of racism. Today's immigrants are largely non-white in a society in which race has been a most significant marker of privilege. When combined with the tentativeness of contemporary, postindustrial job markets for launching successful, secure lives, will limitations of opportunity combine with racial prejudice and discrimination to deny immigrants and their children access to the mainstream, and doom them to permanent poverty and social marginality? Such observers have ventured to project that if so, many immigrants will experience a different type of assimilation, a downward *segmented assimilation*. Rather than upward mobility, they will fall permanently into the urban underclass, residing in the crime-infested, drug-ridden ghetto-slums of the nation's decaying inner cities, which they will share with poor African Americans. They will make a living on the wrong side of the law for want of alternatives, or they will depend on expensive, tax-supported social assistance programs, which contemporary local and state governments can no longer afford.

Testing pessimistic scenarios

Nightmare visions aside, historic assimilation patterns have been thoroughly analyzed in a number of studies based on massive sets of quantitative data and, most importantly, a variety of systematic comparisons, using comparable historical and contemporary data, between ethnic groups in the past and those in the present. Joel Perlmann, one of the most thorough of these investigators, and other researchers have summarized the results of these investigations:

1. Just as in the past, there are such profound differences among and within the diverse contemporary immigrant groups that it is not possible to generalize about the category "immigrant."

2. Not all contemporary immigrants are poor and bring low skill sets; a substantial number possess academic and technical education and job skills when they arrive in the United States.

3. While high-wage, machine-tender factory jobs are in shorter supply than at the time of the second great immigration wave, low-skill work, including factory employment, exists in sufficient volume to employ many unskilled immigrants with steady work in times of economic prosperity.

4. Just as was true for many of the children of the second-wave immigrants in the early twentieth century, educational advancement continues to support upward mobility, and a number of contemporary immigrant groups have demonstrated a commitment to using education for credentialing and have attained stability in white- and blue-collar jobs.

5. Racial hierarchies are socially and culturally formed and, as in the past, evolve and dissolve over time. Many European immigrants were racialized and found the mainstream, and America's visible minorities (African American, Hispanic, Native American, and Asian American) have unprecedented access to the mainstream today.

6. Crime among youth of immigrant families, and types of segmented assimilation more generally, are hardly new phenomena and, where they have been common, have not proven permanent.

In short, as in the past, there is tremendous variability in the experiences of contemporary individuals and immigrant groups, some achieving stability and prosperity, but some not doing as well. There are those who find themselves, like the Italians of the first half of the twentieth century, accused of failing to assimilate, being mired in poverty and crime, and taxing law-enforcement agencies and social services. It is easy to forget the fear about blocked

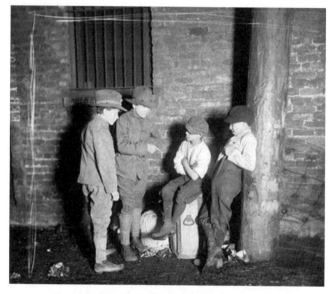

12. Boy Scouts talking to two italian immigrant boys, 1915. Long considered resistant to assimilation, Italian immigrants, like these young street boys, were frequently the targets of Americanizers. As the cued body language of both sets of boys suggests, this photograph seems to have been posed for an American audience of newspaper readers who accepted that view of Italians.

mobility that attached itself especially to the urban working class, Italian immigrants and their American-raised children, and thus inspired such pessimistic sociological studies as William Foote Whyte's *Street Corner Society: The Social Structure of an Italian Slum* (1943). Whyte reported about life in a neighborhood likely to be judged by respectable Americans, as his publisher said in advertising the book, "mysterious, dangerous, and depressing." Some young men dropped out of school, worked irregularly, joined gangs, participated in petty crime, and had troubled relations with police. Other young men, whose lifestyle was less colorful, left school for the industrial workforce, just as young women left school to become wives and mothers. There are few traces of this inner-city, white, working-class ethnic world left today. Instead there are some new immigrants who might be described in the same way.

For Perlmann and others, the critical test case for the possibility that contemporary immigrants will find the mainstream in ways that are historically conventional or will, alternatively, fall victim to downward, segmented assimilation lies in the trajectory of Mexicans, the largest group of contemporary immigrants. Because of the educational credentials, job skills, savings, and tight family and community solidarity many Asians bring to the United States, they are deemed much less problematic. Some analysts project a new, polarized racial hierarchy forming in which Asians join whites of European background at the top of the racial pyramid, and immigrants from the Caribbean and Latin America, especially Mexicans, fit themselves at various levels toward or at the bottom.

Mexicans are also critical to the pessimism of contemporary nativists like Huntington, who predicts that rather than the Americanization of Mexican immigrants, what will evolve in the twenty-first century is the Hispanicization of America, largely because the Mexicans cannot and will not assimilate. The source of this pessimism is a conjunction of related situational factors and political, economic, and social processes. The long land border between the United States and Mexico facilitates a continuing high volume of legal and illegal immigration; Mexicans are concentrated in especially high numbers in southwestern states along that border; and the Mexican immigration, legal and illegal, shows no signs of abating due to the uneven performance of the Mexican economy. Supplemented by constant migrations, Mexicans might well create a world of their own inside the United States. Moreover, Huntington's research yields findings that show that Mexican assimilation lags in language shift, education beyond the primary grades, occupational and income mobility, intermarriage, American identification, and citizenship acquisition.

At the end of this nightmare vision is a restive, disloyal, and unassimilated Mexican population living in isolation in the United States and acting as the subversive wedge for a Mexican irredentism focused on retaking the territory conquered by Americans in the mid-nineteenth century. It is a vision that, alongside the general anxieties about the decline of the white population, helps to animate contemporary nativism. It gives rise to contemporary Americanizers, who campaign for English-only policies, especially in public education, and for repressive state immigration and restrictive public welfare laws that, in turn, breed an angry ideological resistance to assimilation, especially among rebellious ethnic young people.

Yet contemporary and historical research, utilizing official government statistics and local ethnographic surveys, does not yield evidence of a unique social pathology among Mexicans that might lead to a permanent, dangerous underclass, let alone of resistance to assimilation. The importance of Perlmann's research in particular is that he simultaneously undertakes systematic socioeconomic comparisons between the Italian and other European immigrants of a century ago, contemporary African Americans, and recent Mexican immigrants. Like the Italians and others, the Mexican second generation does tend to leave school early for the workforce and for homemaking, at a time when education is crucial for upward socioeconomic mobility. But Mexican American youth have relatively high labor force participation, and research found them to be more likely to be working full time than either American-born whites or American-born blacks. Their income tends to be lower than whites as a consequence of their educational deficit, but higher than that of African Americans. Among Mexicans, relative especially to poor inner-city African Americans, the single mother/missing (or incarcerated) father household is much less prevalent. This relatively greater presence of intact families may help to explain the greater income of Mexican American families when there are working women within them. When Mexican Americans and native whites are at the same level of educational attainment, there is virtual parity in family income.

The policy implications of such findings are that relatively low-cost campaigns encouraging high school graduation and combating job discrimination might significantly impact the prospects for more Mexican Americans joining the mainstream in a timely fashion. More time spent in school would probably increase command of English, but the language deficit is not nearly as dire as often imagined. In 1990 it was found that among the third generation, two-thirds of Mexican American families spoke only English at home. Research also revealed that the percentage of Mexican Americans in the twenty-five to forty-four-year-old cohort speaking English well did not vary greatly whether individuals lived near the border, in a border state, or in the interior of the United States, and was between 95 percent and 98 percent in all three physical locations.

When compared to the southern, eastern, and central European immigrants of a century ago, Mexicans have been progressing more slowly, so that it might take them four or five generations rather than three or four to close the gaps that keep them more on the margins than in the center of the mainstream, but there is nothing essentially Mexican in the situation. Much has to do with the larger society in which they reside and work. The European immigrants of a century ago lived at a time when income inequality was declining, but the gap between the affluent and the rest of society has been growing in America for decades. Moreover, government services to assist parts of the population in need are in decline.

Such findings are not enough around which to base the future of immigration policy. They do not mandate that permanent, large-scale immigration is the best policy. The questions of numbers and criteria for determining who will be admitted must be determined according to projections of economic growth and the social costs of supporting and maintaining the generations of Americans who will see the nation into the future. Such findings do indicate that the most pessimistic conclusions about the future of immigrant assimilation need not determine immigration policy, which should instead be based on constructive calculations about the economic and social interests of both Americans and immigrants. They also suggest that Americans need not consider themselves embarking into the unknown when considering contemporary immigration. In fact, they have confronted mass immigration before, and their society has not only survived but become stronger for the diversity embedded within it.

Yet such findings also suggest the depths of an ongoing crisis that is not sufficiently addressed: the stagnant position of members of America's largest domestic racial minority, African Americans, many of whom are being overtaken and passed by, as immigrants move into the mainstream. It remains a bitter irony in the midst of celebrations of immigrant achievements that programs, such as affirmative action in hiring or in college admissions, which were developed in the mid-twentieth century following civil rights protests to address long-standing institutional racism and to assist African Americans, have been utilized more successfully by non-white immigrants to speed their own entrance into the mainstream. The government has allowed the application of such programs to immigrants of color and their children in the service of the laudable goals of immigrant assimilation and multicultural diversity in workplaces and educational institutions. But the ongoing neglect of their original intentions is no credit to American social policy.

Regardless of partisan viewpoint, American pessimism about immigration is hardly novel. Contemporary pessimism is reinforced by a general mood of gloom about America's economic prospects. Yet in light of the history of the absorptive capacities of American society and the historical dynamism and resiliency of the American economy in generating opportunity, hopefulness in contemplating the future of American diversity is certainly possible.

Conclusion

Americans have built a global society whose peoples' origins have come to look much like the world itself. This is an observation made daily by tourists from outside the United States for whom such symbolic locations at the crossroad of American diversity as New York City's Times Square or the multicultural neighborhoods of America's big cities, such as Chicago, Miami, or Los Angeles, have a cosmopolitan dynamism that seems uniquely American. At eye level these exciting manifestations of multicultural America are not easily forgotten, especially by those residing in more homogeneous societies.

This global society developed in fits and starts. There has never been consensus on whether it should be a national aspiration. It arose while Americans were pursuing another end, the material development of their part of North America. While American diversity certainly has been debated widely in ideological terms, at the heart of its creation was and continues to be a matter that resists moral calculation: the demand for labor to sustain economic development. Like the slave trade, voluntary immigration has been an economic and social investment in human labor, and the cheaper the labor, the more it has been valued. A labor force formed exclusively from native-born American population would not have been large enough to propel the United States into the status of the world's leading economy in the twentieth century. With an aging native-born population at present, there are probably not enough Americans to provide for the country's future needs for workers. Moreover, immigrants are proving vital to the renewal of American cities and, as taxpayers, to the support of government programs.

American debates about immigration have always been rendered more substantively complicated and emotionally fraught to the extent that the *necessary* (labor) and the *good* (homogeneity or heterogeneity) have been tied together, forming a knot that it is very difficult to untie. Over time what came to exist as a result of economic calculation also came to be regarded by many as an object of pride in a way that the slave trade could never be. Even those who stood against the continuation of large-scale immigration might argue that what no longer was beneficial had once been, and represented a venerable history, worthy of respect if no longer of emulation. It has frequently been noted that for many contemporary Americans their own immigrant ancestors, however once berated or loathed by native-born Americans, were hard-working, right-living, God-fearing people who were ideal material for American citizenship—in contrast to contemporary immigrants, whom these same Americans believe embody opposite, negative characteristics.

To be sure, the actual, frequently messy work of forming societies is quite different than the idealistic and patriotic views that come to justify and defend them, and which provide simple, emotionally sustaining explanations for complex developments and a source of national pride. As its immigration history and the mythologies that pass for understanding of that history make clear, America is no different in that regard. Yet its real historical achievement in creating a global society may be its greatest claim to attention and respect.

Further reading

Introduction

Fuchs, Lawrence H. *The American Kaleidoscope: Race, Ethnicity, and the Civic Culture*. Hanover, NH: Wesleyan University Press, 1990.

Gerstle, Gary. *American Crucible: Race and Nation in the Twentieth Century*. Princeton, NJ: Princeton University Press, 2001.

Jacobson, Matthew Frye. *Whiteness of a Different Color: European Immigrants and the Alchemy of Race*. Cambridge, MA: Harvard University Press, 1999.

Roediger, David R. *Working toward Whiteness: How America's Immigrants Became White*. New York: Basic Books, 2005.

Part I

Graham, Otis. *Unguarded Gates: A History of America's Immigration Crisis*. Lanham, MD: Rowman and Littlefield, 2004.

Higham, John. *Strangers in the Land: Patterns of American Nativism, 1860–1925*. New York: Atheneum, 1963.

Kettner, James. *The Development of American Citizenship, 1608–1870*. Chapel Hill: University of North Carolina Press, 1978.

Lee, Erika. *At America's Gates: Chinese Immigration during the Exclusion Era, 1882–1943*. Chapel Hill: University of North Carolina Press, 2003.

Ngai, Mae M. *Impossible Subjects: Illegal Aliens and the Making of Modern America*. Princeton, NJ: Princeton University Press, 2004.

Part II

John Bodnar, *The Transplanted: A History of Immigrants in Urban America.* Bloomington: Indiana University Press, 1985.

Foner, Nancy. *From Ellis Island to JFK: New York's Two Great Waves of Immigration.* New Haven, CT: Yale University Press, 2000.

Gardiner, Martha. *The Qualities of a Citizen: Women, Immigration, and Citizenship, 1870–1965.* Princeton, NJ: Princeton University Press, 2005.

Leavitt, Peggy. *The Transnational Villagers.* Berkeley: University of California Press, 2001.

Reimers, David. *Other Immigrants: The Global Origins of the American People.* New York: New York University Press, 2005.

Part III

Alba, Richard, and Victor Nee. *Remaking the American Mainstream: Assimilation and Contemporary Immigration.* Cambridge, MA: Harvard University Press, 2003.

Kasinitz, Philip, John H. Mollenkopf, Mary C. Waters, and Jennifer Holdaway. *Inheriting the City: The Children of Immigrants Come of Age.* New York: CUNY Press, 2008.

Perlmann, Joel. *Italians Then, Mexicans Now: Immigrant Origins and Second Generation Progress, 1890–2000.* New York: Russell Sage, 2005.

Portes, Alejandro, and Reuben G. Rumbaut. *Legacies: The Story of the Immigrant Second Generation.* Berkeley: University of California Press, 2001.

Index